7000
YEARS

ANDREW MULLEK

Seven Thousand Years
By Andrew Mullek

Copyright © 2016, 2018 Andrew Mullek

Revised Edition: Two New Chapters (11 & 12) Included

Printed by CreateSpace

ASIN: B01MAWIVXJ

Freely we receive, freely we should give.

Contents

Acknowledgements 5

Introduction: Is it Possible? 7

1. Seven Thousand Years 11

2. The Creation Account 13

3. A Day Shall Be Like a Thousand Years.................... 23

4. Adam: Man, Myth, or Monkey? 29

5. Are We Living in the End Times? 35

6. Hidden Treasures 43

7. The Millennial Reign 49

8. Old Testament Shadows 53

9. The Seventh Day 63

10. The Third Day 71

11. Daniel's Seventy 'Sevens' 79

12. What About the Rapture? 87

13. The Seven Festivals of the Messiah – The Spring Festivals.....79

14. The (Unfulfilled) Fall Festivals 105

15. Every Two Thousand Years................................... 111

16. Jesus' Genealogies 117

17. What Now? 121

Appendix 127

Note From the Author 129

Acknowledgements

For from him and through him and for him are all things. To him be the glory forever! Amen

Romans 11:36

Introduction: Is it Possible?

Could it be possible that God outlined mankind's history on the first few pages of His book, only for it to have gone unnoticed for the past six thousand years? What if there was evidence that God gave indicators in the Bible that point to a seven-thousand-year historical timeline, culminating in Jesus' second coming and a thousand-year period of peace?

If so, it would not be the first time in our history that we managed to overlook biblical indicators pointing to Jesus' coming.

Once upon a time, some really smart guys made the greatest discovery ever. It was such an epic and bizarre event that it has become one of our favorite Christmas stories. These guys found God! They discovered Him in an unusual way: they followed a star. What a great scene for a children's play.

When we start to dig a bit deeper into what happened, some questions arise. How did they know where the star would lead? Why did they bring gifts? How could they have known what they would find? There is only one answer to these questions. They had studied the Bible and understood there was a prophecy about a star (Numbers 24:17). They held onto that information in case a star actually appeared. It did. And when it came, they were ready to follow it.

What is most striking is that these were the ONLY people who followed the star. No one else picked up on it. Amazing. God prophesied in the Bible that a star would lead to Jesus and only one small band of guys put the prophecy together with the event.

Others were aware of the prophecies, but they ignored them. The experts of the law knew Jesus would be born in Bethlehem and they knew the Magi were following a star there (Matthew 2:6). Yet, they did not follow the star. Only the Magi managed to understand and believe the significance of the prophetic word about the star.

I suppose the Magi were not one hundred percent sure if a star would ever actually come. As humans, they must have had their doubts. Nevertheless, they held on to the possibility. In the end, the star provided a perfect map that led them directly to Jesus.

I believe God has given us another map within the Bible that points to Jesus' second coming. This work explores the amazing theory that God has mapped out a six-thousand-year timeline for man, culminating in Jesus' second coming and His thousand-year reign. If this is true, then the six thousand years of biblical history are approaching a quick end.

Hundreds of Old Testament prophesies outlined Jesus' first coming in exact detail. This alone is incredible. But even more thought-provoking is that there are three times as many biblical promises of His second coming.[1] What they tell us about this pending event is indeed sobering and worthy of our attention.

There is a very exciting reality that this generation could witness the second coming of Jesus. While this is an extraordinary idea, it is no more extraordinary than waiting for and then following a mysterious star. Just like the first time around, I believe God has provided some amazing clues that cannot be easily ignored.

The future itself will confirm or deny the plausibility of this claim. It is not my aim to put a date to Jesus' return. Such would be a huge mistake. Any person who specifically dates this event

---

1   Tim LaHaye & Jerry B. Jenkins, *Are We Living in the End Times?* (Wheaton, IL: Tyndale House, 2011), 3.

cannot be taken seriously. Jesus himself tells us that no one except the Father knows the exact day or hour of his return, but He does caution us to be aware of the season (Matthew 24:30–35).

Two grievous errors have been made when it comes to the topic of the second coming and the end times. One has been to ignore it totally. Jesus clearly wants us to pay attention to the signs of the times. The other has been to try and predict the specific date, and to give this topic an unhealthy interest. The balance is to be found in the middle. We are to be aware of the season, and we are to be constantly ready for our Lord's return while realizing we will not know exactly when that day will be.

I believe we are now in the season of His return. My goal with this work is not to set a date to the most important event yet to come, but to prepare the church for a very unique and real possibility, and to bring God glory should the near future confirm what His Word seems to strongly suggest.

Chapter One

Seven Thousand Years

The Bible begins the written record of mankind with the act of creation, in which God produced a family for Himself that would dwell with the Lord forever – the Lord's inheritance. Once this six-day act was accomplished, the Lord rested for one day. In this account, a potential pattern emerges that could apply to the ensuing history of man.

The Bible ends with the prophetic vision of a thousand-year reign of Christ, where Jesus dwells with the saints on earth. Is this not the Lord resting after He has possessed his inheritance in the saints, just as He did after creation?

Now this is where the parallel gets interesting:

Bible scholars, who believe in the literal interpretation of creation, postulate that humans have only existed for about six thousand years. This is supported by biblical chronology and even by modern science, which will be explored more in future chapters.

Many believers feel we are living in the end times because of present-day events, such as the fulfillment of prophecy that includes the formal recognition of Israel as a nation, recent increases in natural disasters and the political situation in the Middle East.

If we are actually living in the end times, and the second coming of Jesus is to occur during our lifetime, we could be looking at six thousand years of human existence followed by the second coming and an ensuing one thousand years of rest. The result is a seven-thousand year historical timeline for mankind that would perfectly mirror the timeline for creation.

This is an amazing thought and is given credibility when we consider the biblical emphasis on the number seven as a symbol of perfect completion. Numbers in the Bible often have a specific meaning. For example, the number forty represents the fullness of time. The number seven (along with three) is a number that symbolizes perfection. It is God's number.

The Bible is leading us to a final point in history where man will be reconciled to God. The end will be our eternal dwelling with the Lord.

In the same way, the purpose of creation was for man to dwell in the Garden of Eden with God forever. Are not the two (the history of man and the story of creation) mapping a road where man ultimately ends up as a desired member of the family of God – dwelling with the Lord? At the very least, the creation story and the rest of the Bible point us in the same direction and being purposed for the same end. But there could be significantly more to the parallel.

When we consider that God may have a seven-thousand-year timeline in mind, the story of creation begins to take on new life in terms of a symbolic chronology of all of man's time on earth. Day one of creation corresponds amazingly with the first thousand years of history. Day two corresponds with the second millennia, and so on. The creation account found on first page of the Bible could well be God's perfect blueprint for the history of mankind.

As you'll see in the next chapter, the first two chapters of the Bible actually contain key insights into how this history will unfold.

Chapter Two
The Creation Account

When the possibility of a seven-thousand-year timeline came to me, I was led to consider the creation account. I knew there were six days of creation capped off by a rest day, and it seemed there could be a parallel between each of those days and the recorded six thousand years of mankind's history from Adam, which would be capped off by a millennial rest.

With that in mind, I started to read through the days of creation. The parallels I found between each day of creation and each millennia of history were unmistakable. The most important event of each thousand-year period of history lined up perfectly with its corresponding day of creation. I was shocked to see the history of man outlined on the first page of God's book, and part of me just laughed in marvel at God's sense of humor.

It is my hope in writing this book that you can rejoice with me in a God who does not reveal everything to us at once, but who receives incredible glory and honor when we begin to understand His bigger picture.

DAY 1 – LIGHT AND DARK

And God said, "Let there be light, and there was light. God saw that the light was good, and he separated the light from the darkness. God called the light "day," and the darkness he called "night." And there was evening, and there was morning – the first day. (Genesis 1:3–6)

On the first day, God created light and He separated the day from the night. This event marked the unfolding of history as we know it. But it would seem God was doing more than just setting light and dark into motion. This day of creation foreshadows the key event of the first millennia – Adam and Eve's choice. Just as light and darkness came into being on the first day, so good *and evil* were brought into the world in the first thousand years.

Light and darkness are commonly referred to in the New Testament as symbols for good and evil. Jesus even refers to himself as light, saying "I am the light of the world. Whoever follows me will never walk in darkness, but will have the light of life" (John 8:12).

Some dispute that the first day happened as the Bible said it did. They do so on the grounds that the sun and moon were not created until the fourth day. Thus, there could not have been light and dark on the first day. This is not a problem when we understand that God's very presence produces "light." The book of Revelation describes heaven like this: "The city does not need the sun or moon to shine on it, for the glory of God gives it light, and the Lamb is its lamp" (21:23). It goes on to say, "There will be no more night. They will not need the light of a lamp or the light of the sun, for the Lord God will give them light" (22:5). In other words, God's glory is a radiant light, even producing a light brighter than the sun (Acts 26:13).

We find that the first thousand years deals directly with the influence of light and dark. The first millennium would have been a world coming to grips with spiritual darkness versus spiritual light. Before Adam and Eve ate from the tree of the knowledge of good and evil, all they ever knew was the presence of God and good. But Satan accurately tells Adam and Eve that eating the fruit will allow them to know both good *and evil* (Genesis 3:5). Of course, this happens. They went from knowing only good to knowing both good and evil, and the proverbial battle of light and dark began.

This battle would define Adam's lifetime, which spanned the majority of the first millennium of history. One of the few recorded biblical events that occurred during this period was the murder of Abel, Adam's son. This first thousand years would have been a time where the world was defined by this knowledge, or "darkness." The goodness of Eden was separated from a world under the curse of sin in the very same way that God separated light from darkness on the first day of creation.

DAY 2 – THE WATERS AND THE HEAVENS

God said, "Let there be an expanse between the waters," and He separated the water with an expanse above it – the sky. (Genesis 1:6–7)

The second millennium of human existence began with the birth of Noah. By studying the biblical timeline, we find that Noah was born approximately one thousand years after Adam and Eve, and his life, which lasted 905 years, nearly covered the entire second thousand years. The defining event of the second millennium of human history on earth was the flood, which occurred around 1600 years after Adam and Eve, or 2400 B.C.

Just as day two dealt with water covering the earth, so this time was marked by the same. In direct response to the evil on the earth, God sent the flood to cleanse and repopulate the world with Noah's family.

The second day of creation ends with a separation of the water and the sky, and God ends the flood in the second millennium by promising never to allow water (the floods) to mix with the sky (the judgment of the heavens). The parallel here is incredible. We'll see later how Noah's life actually prefigures the second coming of Jesus.

DAY 3 – SEED BEARING PLANTS

God made land to separate the water, and said, "Let the land produce vegetation: seed-bearing plants and trees on the land that bear fruit with seed in it, according to their various kinds." And it was so. The land produced vegetation: plants bearing seed according to their kinds and trees bearing fruit with seed in it according to their kinds. (Genesis 1:11–12)

The defining event of the third millennia was God's covenant with Abraham. This time period (two thousand years after Adam) began with the birth of Abraham and with God's promise to him to create a nation that would be as numerous as the stars in the sky. Through Abraham, God birthed an entire nation of twelve tribes under what we now call the old covenant.

God actually makes this covenant with Abraham and with his *seed*: "I will greatly bless you, and I will greatly multiply your seed as the stars of the heavens and as the sand which is on the seashore; and your seed shall possess the gate of their enemies. In your seed all the nations of the earth shall be blessed, because you have obeyed My voice" (Genesis 22:17–18 NASB). Almost every time that God speaks to Abraham, he reaffirms the covenant with Abraham's seed.[2] The word used here for seed is the very same word used for seed on day three of creation. The parallel with the third day of creation would seem intentional.

Abraham's offspring became God's chosen people, and the story of their relationship with God takes us to the time of Jesus, when a new covenant was formed. The key events of the third millennia (the establishment of Israel, the bondage in Egypt, the Exodus, the call of Moses, inheriting the Promised Land, etc.)

---

2 Genesis 12:7; 13:15–16; 15:3,5,13,18; 16:10; 17:7–12; 17:19; 21:12–13; 22:17–18

revolve around Abraham's seed and the covenant they had with God.

Abraham's offspring is further referred to in the New Testament as seed: "If you belong to Christ, then you are Abraham's seed, and heirs according to the promise" (Galatians 3:29). In the same way the seed-bearing plants and trees produced vegetation (according to their kind), God began populating the earth with chosen people from the seed of Abraham. During the third millennium, the nations were being formed just as the plants produced fruit "according to their kind," and Abraham's seed set into motion the course of biblical history.

DAY 4 – THE SUN, THE MOON AND THE STARS

And God said, "Let there be lights in the expanse of the sky to separate the day from the night and let them serve as signs to mark seasons and days and years, and let them be lights in the expanse of the sky to give light to the earth." And it was so. God made two great lights – the greater light to govern the day and the lesser light to govern the night. He also made the stars. God set them in the expanse of the sky to give light on the earth, to govern the day and the night, and to separate light from darkness. (Genesis 1:14–19)

The fourth millennium began with the birth of David, and the majority of biblical activity occurred during this time. This period ended with the defining moment of Jesus coming into the world and, I believe, this millennium ultimately ended with Jesus' death and the new covenant. In this period of history, the night represents the time before Jesus and the day is the time after Jesus' first coming.

On day four the sun was created, and near the end of the fourth millennium Jesus was born. His coming was described with the following language: "In him was life, and that life was the light of men. The light shines in the darkness, but the darkness has not understood it…The true light that gives light to every man was coming into the world" (John 1:4,9). Jesus was the true arrival of the "sun" on earth. When Jesus died, the physical sun even stopped shining (Luke 24:45). He called himself the "light of the world" and we are told in Revelation that there is no sun or moon in heaven because God and Jesus are the source of light (21:23).

As New Testament believers, we are told that "We belong to the day" (1 Thessalonians 5:8). Jesus' coming and resurrection allows us to live in the day, while before Him people lived in darkness, governed only by a reflection of Him.

The moon represents the law of Moses, which governed the Israelites during the dark period of history before Jesus came into the world. In the natural, the moon reflects the sun's light, but it is not a source of light. It can only serve to reflect light. In the same way, the law of Moses that governed this time before Jesus was not the source: "The law is only a shadow of the good things that are coming – not the realities themselves" (Hebrews 10:1). The law was merely a mirror that reflected our need for Jesus, just as the moon is a mirror reflecting the reality of the light of the sun.

The stars are also representative of Abraham's descendants, which made up Israel. God promised Abraham in the previous millennium that his descendants would be like the stars in the sky. Among Abraham's children were the many prophets or lights God would send during this time to point the way to Jesus. Both the stars (Israel's prophets) and the moon (the law of Moses) served as sources of light for God's people during the spiritual night of this millennium until the light of the world came into the world at the end of the fourth millennium.

DAY 5 – THE FISH AND THE BIRDS

And God said, "Let the water teem with living creatures,

and let birds fly above the earth across the expanse of the sky." God created the creatures of the sea and the creatures of the air, telling them to "be fruitful and increase in number and fill the water in the seas and let the birds increase on the earth." (Genesis 1:20, 22)

I believe the fifth millennium began after Jesus' death, which is significant in terms of how this relates to the fifth day of creation. Day five was unique. It was the first day God gave a command for something to increase and fill the earth.

The period of history that began after Jesus' death was marked by a very similar command. Jesus' final words to his followers were to increase and fill the earth by going and making disciples of all nations (Matthew 28:19). What we know as "The Great Commission" was the defining purpose of the church after Jesus' death, and it parallels the command God gave the birds and the fish. This was such an important task that Jesus promised He will not return until the gospel is preached to all nations (Matthew 24:14).

The disciples were empowered to fulfill this command to spread Christianity to the ends of the earth when the Holy Spirit (often depicted as a dove as in Matthew 3:16) came upon them with fire on Pentecost, and these fishermen became *fishers* of men. I don't think it is a coincidence that Christians at the beginning of the fifth millennium chose the symbol of the *fish* to represent their belief in Christ.

An interesting event occurred after Jesus rose from the dead. He told his followers to go into Galilee where they would see Him (Matthew 28:10). While there, they were fishing one night and caught nothing. Without them recognizing Him, Jesus appeared and instructed them throw their net on the right side of the boat and they would find some fish. When they did so, they caught 153 LARGE fish (John 21:6–11). Remarkably, the net did not break. In that moment, they recognize Jesus.

Some scholars believe Jesus was giving His followers a picture of their new commission. It is believed that at the time of Jesus there were 153 nations, hence the LARGE fish. Thus, this moment was a prophetic insight as to what Jesus wanted his followers to do. The gospel was given to the disciples to spread to the entire world … to all the nations (Matthew 28:11). They were to become fishers of all nations.

This thousand-year period witnessed the spread of the gospel across the earth. It multiplied as it went and it filled the earth just as the birds and the fish multiplied and filled the air and the seas. God commanded the fish and birds to multiply and subdue the earth, and Jesus commanded us to do the same!

DAY 6 – LIVING CREATURES, MAN AND DOMINION

God said, "Let the land produce living creatures according to their kinds." Then God said, "Let us make man in our own image, and let them rule over the fish of the sea and the birds of the air, over the livestock, over all the earth, and over all the creatures that move on the ground." (Genesis 1:24, 26).

On the sixth and final day of creation, man was made in the image of God and was given dominion over all the animals on earth. After Adam named the creatures, he was still without a suitable partner, at which point God produced Eve from Adam, hence the name "woman" (meaning *from man*).

This last period of history is where we are now, and is defined by man's clear dominance on the earth. Never before have humans exercised such authority over their elements. We have even stretched our reach into space. Rapid advances in technology in this generation have left us with more power than at any other time in the history of the world. The last twenty years have placed us in a position no one could have dreamed possible in previous generations. Yet, the more dominion we gain, the less content we seem to be. Instead of making our lives more comfortable, modern technologies seem to have an adverse effect. At the peak of human power and authority, it is surprising how unhappy most people are.

We share much in common with Adam, who spent the sixth day of creation naming the animals. Though Adam was completely in control of the elements around him, he was lonely and empty at the end of the day.

Just as Adam could not find a suitable partner in his role as the caretaker of the living animals, we will fail to find completion in our role as the caretakers of the things of this world. We were destined to live in union with the Lord. We are His bride, whom He has been preparing to receive. This period will end with the second coming of Christ and the joining of Christ and the church (his bride) just as Adam was joined with Eve. This is what we were made for and, like Adam, our spirit will settle for nothing less.

DAY 7 – GOD RESTED

By the seventh day God had finished his work he had been doing; so on the seventh day he rested from all his work. And God blessed the seventh day and made it holy, because on it he rested from all the work of creating that he had done. (Genesis 2:2–3)

Jesus promised that when He returns there will be a thousand-year period of rest (Revelation 20:1–3), which we'll look at in more detail later. Just as God spent the seventh day resting with His children, so the final millennium will be a period of rest from the forces of evil, where all children on earth will reign with Him.

ETERNITY AFTERWARDS

This will begin a period much like the beginning of time in the Garden of Eden, where Adam dwelt with God and did not know sin. Just as the seven days ended with man placed in the garden of Eden, so too will our time on earth end with man dwelling with God, where Satan will be bound and his rule over the earth will be ended.

Chapter Three
A Day Shall Be Like a Thousand Years

I will never forget the day I felt the Lord download the information I have just shared with you. It happened in a matter of minutes. I was totally stunned by the reality of what I was seeing on the first page of my Bible.

In my excitement, I quickly opened up a book regarding end times prophecy. In that moment I wanted to know just how likely Jesus was to return during our lifetime. Were there any other clues? The possibility of a seven-thousand-year timeline was so real that I needed to know just how much evidence there was that we could be living in the end times.

I opened *Are We Living in the End Times?* to a random page in the book.[3] The first thing I saw was a verse I was completely unfamiliar with. At the time (2005), I was only two years old in the Lord and still growing in my basic Bible knowledge. The verse was this: "With the Lord a day is like a thousand years, and a thousand years are like a day" (2 Peter 3:8). I was absolutely amazed that God immediately confirmed with His Word the very discovery He was quickening to my spirit. Had it not been for that moment, I am not sure whether I would have had the confidence to pursue such an outrageous idea. It is because

---

3   LaHaye & Jenkins, *Are We Living In The End Times?*

of His confirmation that I have acted in faith to share this work with you.

This verse literally blew me away. It spoke everything I had just felt the Lord say to me. I am sure many of us can relate to those special moments when God's Word just jumps off the pages. It is one of the most amazing and beautiful things when God uses His Word to confirm what His Spirit is saying.

The question I'd like us to consider is whether this verse could be taken literally. Is it possible that one day really is meant to be like a thousand years? There are two times this concept appears in Scripture and I believe both support the idea of this book.

PSALM 90:4

The first time this verse appears is in Psalm 90:4: "For a thousand years in your sight are like a day that has just gone by, or like a watch in the night." This is a particularly significant Psalm because it is the one Psalm we know Moses wrote. This is important because scholars believe Moses also wrote Genesis, which included the creation account. Since Moses was not present during creation, there are really only a few ways he would have known what to write. In fact, no one was there except God. The only way anyone could have known about how God created the world was through divine revelation.

God may have given Adam a revelation regarding the days of creation preceding him, and it could have been passed down through oral tradition. This is entirely possible, especially considering the lifespans of people during that time, and the effectiveness of oral tradition in Jewish culture. We tend to overlook the possibility of Biblical events being transferred orally, but we need to keep in mind just how much of the Bible the Israelites were taught to memorize. Jewish children were able to memorize the first five books of the Bible by the time they were twelve. The creation account is only a few chapters out of the 197 chapters found in Genesis through Deuteronomy.

God may also have revealed the Creation account to Moses through a vision or through speaking to him or through some other means. This should not be a problem theologically for anyone who is a believer. Much of the Bible is actually an account of God revealing himself to a person. Either way, Moses was aware of the Creation story and was the one to record it. He was also the first person to write down that "a thousand years in your sight are like a day that has just gone by." I find it remarkable that the same person who was given divine insight to the six days of creation also links a single day to a thousand years in the sight of God.

Psalm 90 actually begins by speaking of God existing before creation. Moses says God was from "everlasting to everlasting." This could only come from God. Moses is speaking about God pre-existing recorded history and existing forever *after* recorded history. He is giving us an insight into the nature of God that extends beyond history on either side, *and* while doing so, Moses links a day to a thousand years. If anyone else in the Bible did this, we would have less reason to take the connection literally.

Furthermore, Moses gives us a prophetic nugget of gold in defining the length of a generation as being seventy or eighty years (Psalm 90:10). We'll see later how that provides a time frame to work from regarding the final generation, and how that verse is often used in the study of Jesus' return.

2 PETER 3:8

The other time this verse emerges is in Peter's second letter: "But do not forget this one thing, dear friends: With the Lord a day is like a thousand years, and a thousand years are like a day" (3:8). It seems a little unusual that in all of his writing to the church, Peter tells his audience not to forget this one concept. What is even more compelling is that this verse comes in the middle of a chapter where Peter is talking about the return of Jesus. This chapter contains statements like:

"... you must understand that in the *last days* scoffers will come scoffing and following their own evil desires. They will say, 'Where is *this coming* he promised?'" (2 Peter 3:3–4)

After that statement, Peter talks about creation, and then speaks about the final judgment, cautioning us not to forget that a day is like a thousand years. This is followed by more verses about the second coming:

The Lord is not slow in keeping his promise, as some understand slowness. He is patient with you, not wanting anyone to perish, but everyone to come to repentance. But the day of the Lord will come like a thief. The heavens will disappear with a roar; the elements will be destroyed by fire, and the earth will be laid bare. Since everything will be destroyed in this way, what kind of people ought you to be? You ought to live holy and godly lives as you look forward to the day of God and speed its coming. That day will bring about the destruction of the heavens by fire, and the elements will melt in the heat. But in keeping with his promise we are looking forward to new heaven and a new earth, the home of righteousness. (2 Peter 3:9–13)

I included this entire passage so we could see that this section of Peter's letter was talking very specifically about the end of the world and the second coming of Jesus. Nestled in between all of these verses about the end of the world and a reference to creation is Peter's admonition to remember that "a day is like a thousand years, and a thousand years are like a day." The context is clearly the end of the world. In fact, this verse is sandwiched between two verses (2 Peter 3:7 and 2 Peter 3:9) that specifically speak of Jesus' coming. It would seem Peter is giving us a clue to what to look out for – one he does not want us to forget.

The parallelism in this verse also seems to stress a more literal understanding of these words. It would be easier to approach the verse figuratively if it *only* said that a day is like a thousand years, but it does not. It goes on to say that a thousand years is like a day.

I believe that not only are we to take these words literally, but Peter and Moses are giving us the context in which they apply: Creation and the Second Coming. The premise of this book falls apart if the context changes, but the context not only fits the theory of this work, it seems to mandate it!

A day shall be like a thousand years and a thousand years shall be like a day. Is this to be our star in the sky? We will later see that this very verse was used by the Jews during Passover in anticipation of the *first* coming of Jesus. Until further notice, I am going to be on the lookout as to whether this is the star we are to be watching out for. As we consider the amazing possibility that a day really could be the same as one thousand years, it is my prayer that this chapter will excite you in increasing measure about Him who was, and who is, and who is to come!

Chapter Four
Adam: Man, Myth, or Monkey?

L et's go back to "the beginning."
A critical question needed to establish a six thousand year historical timeline is, "Can we use Adam as a starting point for human history?" If so, we can estimate six thousand years of history, give or take, between then and now. If we consider the best history book at our disposal, the Bible, we can draw three conclusions about Adam: he existed, he was a man, and he was the first man.

The most obvious proof that Adam was the first man comes from the Genesis creation account (1:26–2:25). Sadly, there has been a tendency in some circles to relegate the book of Genesis to a mythical account. It does, after all, contain difficult concepts to understand in our day, such as a worldwide flood, people who live to be over nine hundred years old, the Garden of Eden, and a single couple through whom God populates the earth. But an honest study of the rest of Bible shows that even the New Testament writers took Genesis literally and they clearly considered Adam to be the first created person.

One of the most important passages of Scripture that establishes Adam's nature as the first man comes not in Genesis, but in Luke's gospel account. Luke was a medical doctor who understood the importance of details. For him, small details made a big difference, as they showed the validity of his testimony about

Jesus. Luke gives us a genealogy of Jesus that traces his lineage all the way back to Adam, clearly establishing Adam as a real person. Furthermore, Luke implies that Adam was the first person, by ending his genealogy with "the son of Seth, the son of Adam, the son of God" (Luke 3:38).

Another verse that points to Adam being the first man is found in Acts 17:26: "From <u>one</u> man he [God] made every nation of men, that they should inhabit the whole earth."

Paul likewise confirms Adam as the firstborn among creation. In his letter to the Romans, he tells us that sin entered the world through <u>one</u> man, and that death was the result of sin, which started from the time of Adam (5:12–14). This poses great theological problems for those who want to blend macro-evolution and a Christian worldview. According to Paul, nothing died before Adam, and Adam was created as a man. Everything that was created by God remained alive until Adam sinned. The garden of Eden was a place where nothing died! In other words, Adam was not the first super-monkey in a chain of previously evolving monkeys.

In terms of human history, we are able to use Biblical genealogies and dates to approximate the total time from Adam until now as being around six thousand years. With this in mind, some incredible Biblical patterns start to emerge. For example, there is exactly a two-thousand-year gap between Adam and Abraham, when God gave his first covenant with Israel. There is then another two-thousand-year gap between Abraham and Jesus, when God gave a new covenant that extended to the Gentiles. And we are currently on the cusp of the next two thousand years from Christ, where I believe we can again anticipate a "new covenant" or dispensation.

WHAT DOES SCIENCE SAY?

If you have read this far, I would guess that one of your biggest questions is "What about the science?" Remarkably, there is a great deal of scientific observation that supports the idea of six thousand years of human history.

Before we look at that, however, we need to understand that some of what we call science is actually conjecture. It is not factual. Evolutionary science contains vast amounts of guess work and bias. In fact, I do not even call "evolution" science. I call it faith. Much of what passes for science is not the result of testing *observable* data. Sadly, it has been labeled "science" and has been accepted as factual, but in many cases it is someone's opinion.

Do you remember the famous icon of evolution of apes slowly "evolving" into man? These images were not the result of scientific evidence. They were the result of people's imagination. No one ever took a photo of Neanderthal man. Ultimately, the amount of forgery that went into that icon was criminal and appalling. I would encourage you to investigate things like this. One of the pictures of Nebraska man, for example, was fabricated based on a single piece of fossil evidence: the tooth of a pig. In other words, some guy went out looking for a missing link, and couldn't find it, so he used a pig's tooth to make one up. He then drew a picture of the half ape/half human and told the world about his incredible discovery. The missing links are still missing.[4]

What few Christians seem to understand is that there is a great amount of scientific evidence to support biblical creation. We have just not been exposed to it. In the last century, the church ceded a great deal of ground on this issue by failing to see the evidence that did support Scripture.

Creation.com is a ministry that explains the science that supports a creationist worldview and a six-thousand-year timeline. One article on the website puts forth 101 scientific evidences for a young earth and for six thousand years of history. The following are just a few of the points they have been able to make using

---

4   *The Creation Answers Book*, p. 123

genuine scientific research that is marked by *observable* data.[5]

- DNA in "ancient" fossils. DNA extracted from bacteria that are supposed to be 425 million years old brings into question that age, because DNA could not last more than thousands of years.
- The ages of the world's oldest living organisms, trees, are consistent with an age of the earth of thousands of years.
- Carbon-14 in coal, oil, fossil wood, and diamonds all suggests ages of thousands of years, not millions.
- The recession of the moon from the earth at the current rates would be catastrophic if we use a timeline with billions of years.
- The rate of change of Saturn's rings indicates a young age.

Human anthropology further indicates that people have only been living on earth for six thousand years, just like the Bible outlines. Agriculture is too recent (less than ten thousand years), human history is too short (four to five thousand years) and there are not nearly enough "stone age" skeletons.[6] Still, we are led to believe that humans have mysteriously been around for one hundred thousand years without using agricultural techniques, without writing and without leaving behind fossil evidence. The biblical account is simply more feasible and *believable*. When you really look at what evolutionists are proposing, it takes more faith to believe the universe burped us out four billion years ago than it does to believe God created the heavens and the earth just as His word says. My point with this section is simple: there is evidence to support the theory of this book.

Science is not at odds with Christianity. I am confident that

---

5   http://creation.com/age-of-the-earth

6   http://creation.com/evidence-for-a-young-world

the more we investigate genuine, provable science through reputable sources like creation.com, the more faith we will have in the God who uses His creation to reveal Himself to His people (Romans 1:20).

Chapter Five

Are We Living in the End Times?

If we can approximate a six-thousand year history from Adam to the present day, the question that naturally follows is, "Are we living in the end times?" If so, then a seven-thousand-year timeline is very feasible.

In answering this question, two points should be re-emphasized: 1) Jesus told us no one knows the *day* of His coming, except the Father (Matthew 24:36) while in the same discourse 2) he cautions us to be aware of the *season* (Matthew 24:32–33). It is a profound thought that while we are not to predict the date of the second coming, we are urged to understand the season of His return.

The believers of Jesus' day failed to understand the signs of His first coming, for which he rebuked them, saying, "You know how to interpret the appearance of the sky, but you cannot interpret the signs of the times" (Matthew 16:3). Many have reacted to date-setting extremists by ignoring Jesus' other words about end-time events, but this is clearly not His intent for His people. Jesus wants us to be aware of the season we are in, and He gives us specific signs to look for.

Just as with the first coming, several prophetic portions of Scripture are meant to prepare believers for the season of the second coming of Jesus. When we consider these, we find several key events have happened that would indicate we have great reason to anticipate Jesus' return within our lifetime.

ISRAEL BECAME A NATION IN 1948

Jesus tells us that the <u>generation</u> that witnesses specific-end time events will also witness His second coming (Luke 21:32, Matthew 24:34). For many Bible scholars, the countdown to Jesus' return began when Israel became a nation in 1948 and when Israel retook Jerusalem in 1967. This miraculously fulfilled a number of prophecies that said the Jews would return to their homeland. Most prophecy scholars believe that the <u>generation</u> that witnessed this would be the final generation (Luke 21:24, 32). This would be our generation.

The length of a generation in Scripture is left intentionally vague. Still, do you remember how Moses defined a generation in Psalm 90 when he spoke about a thousand years being like a day? In that Psalm, he said a generation was seventy or eighty years (Psalm 90:10). Adding eighty years to when Israel became a nation puts us at the year 2028, which is as close as we can estimate to being two thousand years from the death of Christ.

As far back as the seventeenth century, men such as Isaac Newton were linking the coming of Christ with the formation of Israel as a nation ... *before it ever happened.* Newton believed the return of the Jews to Israel and their conversion would "serve to usher in the Millennium." With astounding accuracy, Newton used Daniel 9 to predict Israel would become a nation in 1944 and the end would come between 2,000 and 2,050. "Newton also cites the ancient Jewish and Christian tradition that this world would continue for six millennia and links the end of this period with the creation of the new heaven and earth."[7] Newton's writing

---

7   S. Snobele, "The Mystery of this Restitution of All Things," https://isaacnewtonstheology.files.wordpress.com/2013/06/isaac-newton-on-the-return-of-the-jews.pdf

supports the premise of this theory. He held to a six-thousand-year timeline followed by the coming of Christ and he believed biblical prophecy placed Israel's return as a nation as a defining moment that would usher in the end times.

NATURAL SIGNS

In His teaching on the end times, Jesus tells us that famines and earthquakes will serve as the beginning of the birth pains of the end times (Matthew 24:7–8). Since they are compared with birth pains, it would seem that earthquakes and famines and other natural disasters will become more intense and frequent the closer we get to the end.

I found some very good information from the U.S. Geological Survey, which has compiled data on earthquakes from 1900 until today.

The past decade (2001 – 2010 AD) experienced <u>more major</u> earthquakes than any decade in the previous century. Three of the seven worst earthquakes since 1900 (almost half) have come in the past twelve years:

- Sumatra at 9.1 on the Richter scale in 2004.
- Japan at 9.0 on the Richter scale in 2011.
- Chile at 8.8 on the Richter scale in 2010.

Furthermore, the earthquakes in Sumatra and Japan recorded the most fatalities of any earthquakes during the past 110 years.[8]

Just as Jesus said, we are beginning to see an increase in natural disasters all over the world, and this doesn't end with earthquakes. For example, in January 2012, Hoedspruit, South Africa (my wife's hometown), was flooded following a monsoon. Water

---

8   http://earthquake.usgs.gov/earthquakes/eqarchives/year/mag8/
     magnitude8_1900_date.php.

levels far exceeded the hundred-year flood mark. Nothing like this has ever happened before that anyone can remember. This story is hardly isolated. Many of us have witnessed natural disasters that were inconceivable just twenty years ago.

While there can be no certainty about the day of Jesus' return, I agree with the conclusion that LaHaye and Jenkins make: "Our generation has more reason to believe He [Jesus] could return in our lifetime than any generation preceding us."[9] If it is the case that we are living in the end times, then the six-thousand year timeline is indeed possible. As we explore other biblical indicators (Messianic Feasts, the Millennial Reign, the Sabbath, the third day, etc.), an incredible amount of biblical evidence emerges to support the theory that God preordained a six-thousand-year historical timeline for man followed by a one-thousand-year millennial reign to perfectly complete a seven-thousand-year timeline.

PETER'S PROPHECY AND EVOLUTION

Speaking of the last generation, there is a remarkable prophecy mentioned in 2 Peter about the end times. It just so happens that this prophecy is found the same chapter where we read: "With the Lord a day is like a thousand years, and a thousand years are like a day" (2 Peter 3:8)! The fact that the context of this verse is the second coming of Jesus is something we should carefully consider.

This chapter of Scripture contains one of my favorite end-time prophecies. Peter says that "in the last days scoffers will come, scoffing and following their own evil desires" (2 Peter 3:3). This verse would seem to characterize any number of previous generations, as there have always been scoffers. However, the

---

9   Tim LaHaye & Jerry B. Jenkins, *Are We Living in the End Times* (Wheaton, Il: Tyndale House Pub., 1999), 61.

following verse is very specific to our generation: "But they deliberately forget that long ago by God's word the heavens existed and the earth was formed out of water and by water" (2 Peter 3:5). Peter prophesied that in the last days people would choose to forget that God created the world. Only in this generation have we *deliberately forgotten* that God created the world, as schools and people have adopted evolution as their new faith-based system in the last fifty years or so. Around the time that Israel became a nation, we abandoned the truth in our hearts that God created the world.

To deliberately forget means to know the truth and to choose something else. We all know that God created the world. As stated by the Apostle Paul writing to the Roman church, creation reveals a Creator. I cannot look at a chair and ignore the idea that there was a designer any more than I can look at nature and ignore its designer – God (Romans 1:21). Yet Peter tells us that in the last days, people will make such a choice. In his time, this was unthinkable. One hundred years ago, this was unthinkable. And yet, we have seen it come to pass just as he said it would nearly two thousand years ago. For close to six thousand years, humans have understood the nature of God through creation. Only in recent years has this fundamental principal been ignored and forgotten in what is a remarkable fulfillment of 2 Peter 3:5. As a result, I believe we can conclude we are "in the last days."

OTHER PROPHECIES FULFILLED IN OUR GENERATION

Unlike any before it, the current generation has witnessed the fulfillment of an incredible number of biblical prophecies, which would further indicate we are in the end times. I have listed some of these prophecies, which were put together online by Terry Malone. [10]

---

10 Used with permission from http://www.calvaryprophecy.com/q1044. html.

- The re-gathering of the Jews into their homeland (Ezekiel 37:11–13) after thousands of years of God-ordained exile. Another amazing fact: after thousands of years living in other nations, their Jewish culture has remained intact.

- The rebirth of Israel as a nation in 1948 (Ezekiel 37:10–14; Isaiah 43:5, 6; 66:7–8) in one day. Following their declaration of statehood, the next day five Arab nations attacked Israel. But Israel defeated them and has grown into a major world military power. This prophecy of rebirth essentially kicked off the beginning of the last generation.

- The desert land of Israel will bloom again during this last generation (Luke 21:29–31; Isaiah 41:18–21). This has happened in our lifetime. Israel was a worthless desert place while the Arabs occupied the land. However, once Israel reclaimed their homeland, it has become a fertile oasis.

- A Middle East peace plan with Israel, where Jerusalem is considered a major stumbling block, will develop in the last days (Daniel 9:27; Zechariah 12:3). This is taking place today.

- This peace plan with Israel will ultimately have a seven-year time limit (Daniel 9:27). Right now, virtually every proposed Middle East peace proposal has a timeline within which peace must be realized. The splitting of Jerusalem is usually the final jewel of every peace accord.

- An eastern nation capable of fielding a two-hundred-million man army (Revelation 9:16) will arise during the tribulation period. No nation has ever been able to field an army of this magnitude until this generation (China & India).

- Russia, Iran, a host of northern African nations, and the surrounding Islamic world will forge an alliance and attack Israel (Ezekiel 38 & 39). Today, virtually all of these nations (listed in Ezekiel 38) are already in an alliance with each other.

- In the last days, knowledge will increase dramatically (Daniel 12:4). There is no debating the fact that knowledge has increased by leaps and bounds over the last hundred years, but particularly during the last seventy to eighty years. Medicine and technological discoveries have exploded in this last generation.

I understand that linking all of these scriptures may seem like a stretch. I can assure you it is no less of a stretch than what the Magi were willing to take when they read the following verse in Numbers 24:17 and started linking Jesus' coming to a star in the sky: "I see him, but not now; I behold him, but not near. A star will come out of Jacob; a scepter will rise out of Israel." Nor are these any more far-fetched than the prophetic fulfillments gospel writers pointed out when they spoke of how Jesus fulfilled Old Testament prophecy.

A word of caution: Please do not read this and go into "fear mode" and join a "prepper" community, unless that is something the Lord directs you to do. If God is directing you, I believe He will do so from a place of peace not paranoia. God did not give us signs of His coming in order to scare us. He gave them to us so we would be effective in the season in which we find ourselves. There is way too much fear-mongering in the body of Christ over these things already. The purpose of this chapter is simply to establish that we could be in the end times. Should this be the case, God will give us the wisdom to be effective without our having to live in a state of anxiety and fear.

Chapter Six
Hidden Treasures

The best engagement story I have heard was when my brother's friend, Kyle, proposed to his girlfriend, Jillian. They started dating in high school and had been in a relationship for five years. On their first-year anniversary, Kyle gave Jillian a jewelry box. The jewelry box turned out to be more significant than Jillian initially realized.

On their fifth anniversary, Kyle told Jillian her present was under one of the drawers of that jewelry box. When she removed the drawer, she found a letter taped to the bottom that Kyle had written and dated exactly four years earlier. In that old letter, Kyle told Jillian she was the love of his life and he asked her to marry him. That letter had been sitting in her room for years and Jillian never even knew it. Can you imagine how Jillian must have felt when she read the words of Kyle's proposal that were within reach the entire time?

Only Kyle knew the letter existed, and he waited until just the right time to tell Jillian that there was more in the jewelry box than she was aware of. All who knew Kyle were amazed at his plan "from the beginning" and it was so clear that his intentions were indeed good. One can only imagine just how much this discovery deepened Jillian's affection and love for Kyle.

Kyle hid this engagement letter in his gift of the jewelry box on purpose. God does the same thing with the jewelry box of His

Word. Sometimes He shows us things at a certain time, as if to say, "I have been waiting all along to show this to you." On the day I first linked the days of Creation to our historical timeline, I felt the Lord say to me, just as Kyle did to Jillian, "It was there the whole time." I am blown away by Kyle's and Jillian's story, and I am even more undone by the prospect of God mapping his story (History) on the first page of the Bible.

There are numerous Biblical examples where sections of the Bible contain jewels not immediately seen or understood. When they are more closely examined, we walk away amazed at His plan "from the beginning" and our love for God and His ways deepen.

It is amazing to consider just how often Jesus operates this way. On multiple occasions, He intentionally chose not to reveal the true meaning or treasure behind what He was saying. Jesus did this knowing a day would come when what He said would be understood. His followers would then look back and marvel at His true meaning. Several portions of Scripture contain events that are understood and interpreted by Jesus' followers only in hindsight. In looking at a few examples, we can gain great insight into the ways of a God who takes pleasure in revealing treasures at just the right time.

One of the more overt times Jesus hid something is found in Luke 24:15–16. Two of his disciples were walking and talking about Jesus when "Jesus himself came up and walked along with them; but they were kept from recognizing him." They explained to Jesus that they were confused because there was a prophet (Jesus of Nazareth) who was crucified and buried. They told Him that some women they knew were claiming they'd seen visions and angels and that His tomb was empty. Throughout the conversation, they had no idea they were talking to Jesus until a key moment when he broke bread and their eyes were opened (Luke 24:30–32).

Jesus "hid" himself from these two men for a purpose. We

read that once these men recognized Jesus and He disappeared from their midst, they realized their hearts were burning while he spoke to him and "opened up the Scriptures" (Luke 24:32). What had been closed off to them was opened in a particular moment and they had "burning hearts" as a key to recognize this in the future. By hiding himself, Jesus was helping these men to understand how to hear His voice in their hearts! God always has a purpose in hiding something for a later time. As we'll see, the purpose brings Him great honor and glory and it draws us into a deeper relationship with the Father.

"THIS IS THAT"

Often times God is setting us up for a "this is that" moment. By this I mean that we have a moment where we come to understand what God meant by something He said or did previously. For example, when Pentecost happened, Peter stood up and referred to Joel's prophetic word, basically saying, "This is that" (Acts 2:16).

Let's consider another passage from John:

> Then the Jews demanded of him, "What miraculous sign can you show to us to prove your authority to do all this?" Jesus answered them, "Destroy this temple, and I will raise it again in three days." The Jews replied, "It has taken forty-six years to build this temple, and you are going to raise it in three days?" But the temple he had spoken of was his body. After he was raised from the dead, his disciples recalled what he had said. Then they believed the Scripture and the words that Jesus had spoken. (John 2:18–22)

Jesus was heavily criticized for this comment about the temple. It was one of the key testimonies used to convict and crucify him (Mark 14:57–59). In fact, it was the only thing the

Pharisees could get witnesses to come close to agreeing on. Even then, when this comment was presented at Jesus' trial, He did not clarify the matter, nor did He explain himself to His disciples. He was content to keep the meaning of His words "hidden."

Only after Jesus' death, when it was "too late," did his disciples understand what He meant. Notice the outcome: "they believed the Scripture and the words that Jesus had spoken." Surely His followers already believed Him as well as the Scriptures. Still, when they connected Jesus' words about the temple to His resurrection, their beliefs were deepened. Suddenly, they had a "this is that" moment and their faith grew. God seems willing to let things go undiscovered in order that He may receive glory when they are fulfilled.

Luke's gospel contains two moments where Jesus spoke about His upcoming death, wherein Luke specifically mentions that Jesus' meaning was kept *hidden* from His followers. Luke 9:44–45 says that "While everyone was marveling at all that Jesus did, he said to his disciples, 'Listen carefully to what I am about to tell you: The Son of Man is going to be betrayed into the hands of men.' But they did not understand what this meant. It was *hidden* from them, so that they did not grasp it, and they were afraid to ask about it." Similarly in Luke 18:31–33, Jesus goes into detail about His death, resurrection and the fulfillment of Scripture but "The disciples did not understand any of this. Its meaning was *hidden* from them, and they did not know what he was talking about" (vs. 34).

Again Jesus was content to hide the implication of His words only to have their meaning revealed at a later stage (see Luke 24:6 & 24:45). Imagine the love His followers had for Jesus when they realized He knew about his death and resurrection the entire time. Imagine their wonder at His willingness to *knowingly* make such a commitment to them. This is why God will hide certain things from us. It deepens our awareness of His sovereign plan and our awareness of His love for us. This is why Proverbs tells us, "It is the glory of God to conceal a matter; to search out a matter is the glory of kings" (25:2). God receives glory by hiding certain things for us to discover. He hides things for us, not from us! As we discover what is hidden, we gain a deeper affection for God by becoming more aware of His plan from the beginning.

Much like Kyle had a plan to marry Jillian all along, God had a plan for each of us all along. He also had a plan for His church from the beginning. The Apostle Paul wrote that the riches of the gospel of Jesus to the Gentiles had been *hidden* for ages and generations and was only then being revealed in a glorious way (Colossians 1:25–27 & Ephesians 3:8–9). The discovery of God's glorious plan for the Gentiles brought the early Jewish believers into a place of increased praise for God (Acts 10:18).

If the details of Jesus' death were understood too early, they would have likely brought more confusion than praise. In the context of this book's message, I am excited to consider that God could have hidden a blueprint for the history of His church in the opening words of His jewelry box – the Bible. It makes me want to praise and worship God. I am amazed at His foresight and love for me. I would guess it makes me feel like Jillian must have felt when she took out the drawer of her jewelry box, turned it over, and unfolded a letter written many years ago and saw Kyle's handwriting. She have must thought *"This was there the whole time. He loved me that much. He had a plan all along. What an amazing proposal."*

Jesus is coming back for a bride. This will usher in what we call the Millennial Reign – a honeymoon period between us and Jesus. As we take a closer look at the wedding relationship we are moving towards, it would seem God is revealing treasures that have been stored for thousands of years within His Word! God is like "the owner of a house who brings out of his storeroom new treasures as well as old" (Matthew 13:52).[11] I believe it is His delight to show them to us now.

---

11 While the context of this verse refers to a "teacher of the law who has been instructed about the kingdom," it can also apply to the nature of God.

Chapter Seven
The Millennial Reign

So far we have seen that humans have been living outside of Eden for approximately six thousand years, and that we can potentially expect Jesus to return within the next twenty years. When Jesus does return, the Millennial Reign will take place. This will begin a one-thousand-year period of peace that Jesus will bring to the world before the final judgment (Revelation 20:1–10). According to prophecy, this could occur in our lifetime. If so, then a very intriguing possibility presents itself: we would be looking at a seven-thousand-year history of man, starting with Adam and ending with the final judgment.

Such timing is highly significant in the biblical context, as God loves to use the number seven. This number represents perfection and completion and is found throughout the Bible. In the biblical context, a seven-thousand-year history of man sounds exactly like something God would do. This perfect timeline of human history may well be God's ultimate demonstration of His complete work. As we consider this, a number of puzzle pieces start to take shape and it becomes apparent that God could have laid the framework for this timeline long ago.

The details of what will occur during the millennial reign with Jesus are a very significant piece of this puzzle. This millennium will be distinguished by a time of rest. This allows us to conclude that the millennial reign could be a predestined Sabbath millennium capping off the history of man and the previous six millennia.

The first thing that will usher in rest and peace is that no one alive will have to worry about the devil. Jesus is going to throw the devil in the Abyss and lock him up there, "to keep him from deceiving the nations anymore until the thousand years were ended. After that he must be set free for a short time." (Revelation 20:3).[12] I doubt it is possible, but if we could imagine the world without any measure of evil, we would find ourselves at the starting point of what life with Jesus will be like in His millennial kingdom.

Not only will people not have to worry about temptation, sin and every other form of evil and immorality, but those chosen to live during this time will not die (Revelation 20:6). There will be people living longer than Methuselah, who clocked in as the oldest person in the Bible at 969 years (Genesis 5:27). The ancient joke about being "as old as Methuselah" will have to be re-written.

This will be an unprecedented time in the history of mankind. There will be neither death nor temptation. It is going to be a great gig, and it gets even better. Those alive will have an incredible job description: "they will be priests of God and will reign with him for a thousand years" (Revelation 20:6). For one

———

12 The language here is unmistakable. The writer has no hesitation about generalizing the time the devil will have before the final judgment, but he is very specific regarding the time Jesus will reign with his people. The one-thousand-year timeline here is meant to be taken literally. The reason the devil is going to be set free is that there will be people who are born during this time who will have never been tempted. Those people will need to be given the opportunity to freely choose God. True love always honors freedom of choice. In the same way God let the devil loose in the Garden of Eden, so will He let the devil loose for a short time at the end of Jesus' millennial reign. Every person born in this period will then be given the opportunity to make a choice between God and the devil before the final judgment takes place.

thousand years, those who were faithful during the tribulation (a seven year period of great trial before Jesus' return) will get to hang out with Jesus and reign with Him. Wow.

What excites me the most about this time is the way God describes the earth during this period. We will not be reigning over the earth as we know it. Consider this description:

> The wolf will live with the lamb,
> the leopard will lie down with the goat,
> and the calf and the lion and the yearling together;
> and a little child will lead them.
> The cow will feed with the bear,
> their young will lie down together,
> and the lion will eat straw like the ox.
> The infant will play near the hole of the cobra,
> and the young child put his hand into the viper's nest.
> They will neither harm nor destroy
> on all my holy mountain,
> for the earth will be full of the knowledge of the Lord
> as the waters cover the sea. (Isaiah 11:6–9)

According to this passage, all of the most ferocious animals we can think of will be so peaceful that even children will lead them around and infants will be safe in their presence. This makes sense if we consider that there will be no death. As an animal lover, this is a fascinating portion of Scripture. I can picture children riding around on lions, and I think about what it would be like to swim into the ocean and ride a shark. For that matter, those alive may even be able to breathe under water while doing this, since the second death will have no power over them (Revelation 20:6).

This incredible description gives us just a glimpse of what life in the Messianic Reign will be like. Those living on earth will experience an unimaginable time of peace. After the poetic description above, the very next verse in Isaiah speaks of *rest*: "In that day the Root of Jesse [Jesus] will stand as a banner for the peoples; the nations will rally to him, and his place of *rest* will be glorious" (Isaiah 11:10). The millennial reign will usher in an amazing rest for the earth and its people. Could it be that this is the seventh millennium that fulfills the command calling for a Sabbath rest? The answer to this is very important. If the return of Christ begins a seventh and final millennia, then we can be confident Jesus will return within our lifetime.

In order to fairly answer that question one must first understand two important biblical concepts – the use of "shadows" and the purpose of the seventh day rest (Sabbath).

Chapter Eight
Old Testament Shadows

In the Old Testament, God told his people to do many strange things. He commanded them to observe specific days and feasts without explaining why they were to keep certain days holy or eat certain foods. We can now see that the reason for this was that these were "shadows" God was using to point towards something much bigger.

We saw in chapter six how this presents a profound insight into the character and nature of God. He uses shadows and prophecy to accurately predict the future, and when things happen just as God foretold, He receives immense glory. In the Bible, a shadow is not the main focus. Like a shadow in real life, biblical shadows are prophetic images that outline something real. The only difference is that they precede the real thing. They are a foreshadowing of an important event that still needs to happen, and the Bible is full of them.

A great example of a well-known shadow is the Passover. The Jews were asked to celebrate the Passover when they were being delivered from Egypt. As part of observing this feast, they were told to sacrifice a one-year-old lamb and put its blood on their doorposts. They could not break the bones of the lamb, and the lamb had to be flawless, without defect. If they did this, the angel of death would "pass over" their home and they would be spared (Exodus 12).

As with other regulations, specifics were very important here. God was asking the people to do something that would symbolize a significant future event. The lamb had to be without defect because it represented Jesus who was perfect and without sin (1 Peter 1:19). The Passover was ultimately fulfilled in Jesus, whom John the Baptist refers to as "the Lamb of God, who takes away the sin of the world" (John 1:29). Just as the blood of the lamb saved the Israelites from death, so the blood of Jesus redeems us today.

The Israelites could not break any of the lamb's bones, and we find that none of Jesus' bones were broken on the cross (John 19:36). The legs of the men on either side of Jesus were broken, but Jesus' were not. Even the spear that went through him did not strike bone. It's truly amazing that God knew thousands of years in advance it would happen this way, and He foreshadowed the event of Jesus' crucifixion with the Passover lamb.

To complete the puzzle, God's timing with the Passover Feast was perfectly fulfilled in the specific day and hour that Jesus died. Timing mattered. When God instructed the Israelites about Passover, He gave them specific dates to yearly celebrate the feast. Fifteen hundred years later, Jesus was crucified during the Passover Feast (John 19:14). He died at three o'clock in the afternoon (Mark 15:34), which, as Edward Chumney points out in *The Seven Festivals of the Messiah*, is exactly the same time the Passover lamb was to be sacrificed (Exodus 12:6).[13] It is awe-inspiring to begin to understand how intentional God's timing is, and just how perfectly He puts all of the pieces in place. There is a precedent set forth in Scripture that confirms God foreshadows even the timing of events. Knowing this, we can have a measure of confidence in considering this theory of a seven-thousand year history.

---

13 Edward Chumney, *The Seven Festivals of the Messiah* (Shippensburg, PA: Treasure House, 2001), 29.

Paul comments in the New Testament about Jewish observances similar to the Passover, saying they were a shadow of future events: "Therefore do not let anyone judge you by what you eat or drink or with regard to a religious festival, a New Moon celebration or a Sabbath day. These are a shadow of the things that were to come; the reality, however, is found in Christ" (Colossians 2:16–17).

These observances all find their fulfillment some way in Jesus Christ! The more we dig into the Old Testament, the more we see one big arrow pointing to Jesus. We are mistaken, however, when we believe the arrow only points to the Jesus we see in the gospels. How easily the church forgets Jesus is coming back again. Just as with Jesus' first coming, there are naturally a number of shadows pointing to His return, which will be investigated throughout the remainder of this book.

THE SABBATH – A SHADOW OF THE MILLENNIAL REIGN

One of the most important observances followed by the Israelites was the Sabbath, a seventh day rest that the Jews were commanded to observe. Just as God rested on the seventh day of creation, so the Israelites, their animals and servants were told to rest after six days of work. One can hardly read a section of the Old Testament without finding mention of it. Appearing 170 times in the Bible,[14] the Sabbath was the most prevalent of the Jewish observances. It is outlined in the Ten Commandments; in fact, it is the longest commandment (Exodus 20:8–11).

According to Paul, the Sabbath was a shadow of things to come, and its reality is to be found in Christ (Col. 2:16–17). If the Sabbath is a shadow, what exactly is it a shadow of? How does a seventh day rest find fulfillment in Christ? This is a tremendous

---

14 This number comes from wiki.answers.com.

question, given the theory of this book. I believe this critical regulation was put in place to point toward the millennial rest we would have upon Jesus' second coming, which would take place six thousand years after Adam was removed from Eden.

In order to appreciate the significance of the coming Millennial Reign, we need to understand what life was like before sin. Before Adam's fall, life was great! He was not going to die, and he got to walk around with God all day. My guess is that Adam was also riding lions in the Garden of Eden. Maybe he was even surfing on whales and swimming with sharks.

But when he fell, everything changed and the rest man was intended to enjoy with God ended. The world became a cursed place, and Adam was forced to work for his food by the sweat of his brow (Genesis 3:19). Creation is still under the curse of original sin, which Paul confirmed when he wrote that "creation has been subjected to frustration" (Romans 8:20). In fact, we read that Creation is "groaning" and that it "waits in eager expectation" for the sons of God to be revealed (Romans 8:22 & 19).

One of the verses that emphasizes the curse over creation is when Jesus said that if his followers don't praise Him, the stones will cry out (Luke 19:40). This tells me the rocks have the capacity to praise God. Not only that, but we know the stars sang out God's praises (Job 38:7). Incidentally, science is starting to catch up to Scripture in this regard. NASA has actually recorded music made by stars.[15] It's phenomenal that 21st century science has confirmed something happening in space that was first mentioned in the book of Job, which many consider to be the oldest book in the Bible. Along with the stars and rocks, all of creation is mentioned in Psalm 148 as praising God. Incredible. If you can all of nature and the animal kingdom in a full chorus of praise,

---

15 http://thespiritscience.net/2015/06/15/nasa-discovers-planets-and-stars-give-off-music-this-is-what-it-sounds-like/

then perhaps you can begin to imagine the devastating effects of sin and the devil on our world.

For six thousand years, the earth has been frustrated by the effects of Adam's sin and peace has eluded us as a result. We have remained restless.

This will change, for the curse will be lifted when Jesus returns and we will no longer toil for food. Even the animals will enjoy the benefits of this upcoming rest. Instead of chasing its prey, the lion will eat grass. This is a picture of what life must have been like during Eden. It is God's original design. Creation's restlessness will end with Jesus' coming.

It is wonderful to consider the link between the two words, "rest" and "restored." When our bodies rest, they become restored. This is part of the reason God wants us to take a day off. During the millennial reign, there will be rest and the earth will be restored to its original design – Eden.

The Sabbath rest will find its fulfillment in the millennial reign, and it now seems more possible than ever that this could happen six thousand years from when Adam first sinned and our rest was ended.

ENOCH – A SHADOW OF THE MILLENNIAL REIGN

Enoch initially appears to be little more than an aside in the Bible, but upon closer examination no one represents the coming millennial reign and restoration of God's purpose for man more than he does.

Do you remember Methuselah…the old guy? Enoch was his dad. But there is something far greater that distinguishes Enoch: he walked with God.

When Enoch had lived 65 years, he became the father of Methuselah. And after he became the father of Methuselah, Enoch walked with God 300 years and had other sons and daughters. Enoch walked with God; then he was no more, because God took him away. (Genesis 5:21–24)

I think of Enoch with fondness. I can just see him walking hand in hand with God. When I picture them, he and God are walking in their own direction…away from the things of the world. I so desire this. One of the cries of my heart is that I would experience the same intimacy with God that Enoch had. I believe I was made for this type of relationship, and when I consider God's call on my life, that picture often comes to mind.

Enoch represents all of us. The end result of creation was for God to dwell with men in Eden. Similarly, the end result of this world is for us to dwell with God. The story begins and ends in the same way; we are somewhere in the middle. John Eldredge puts it like this:

It is our deepest need as human beings, to learn to live intimately with God. It is what we were made for. Back in the beginning of our story, before the fall of man, before we sent the world spinning off its axis, there was a paradise called Eden. In that garden of life as it was meant to be, there lived the first man and woman. Their story is important to us because whatever it was they were, and whatever it was they had, we also were meant to have. And what they enjoyed above all the other delights of that place was this – they walked with God. They talked with him, and he with them.

For this you and I were made. And this we *must* recover.[16]

Just as God's desire was to dwell with Adam in Eden, so His desire is to dwell with us in heaven. His purpose in creating us

---

16 John Eldredge, *Walking with God* (Nashville, TN: Thomas Nelson, 2008), ix.

has not changed. When our circumstances changed, God made a plan to reconcile us to Him, so Eden may be attained once again. Enoch's relationship with God was special, but it is not beyond what we should expect for ourselves. It represents what God purposed for each of us, which will come to pass when Jesus returns to restore the earth. During the millennial reign, we will walk with God like Enoch, and like Adam did before he sinned. This also represents our current mandate to see God's kingdom come on earth *as it is heaven*. For more on our present-day mandate to do that, I would strongly suggest you read Bill Johnson's book, *When Heaven Invades Earth*.

Another key detail about Enoch is that he never died. We find that Enoch was no more – God took him away (Genesis 5:24). The book of Hebrews explains this more clearly: "By faith Enoch was taken from this life, so that he did not experience death; he could not be found, because God had taken him away" (11:5). What a picture! This is what should have happened with Adam, and it is a shadow of the millennial reign that is coming where we will walk with God and we too will not experience death. We will just be taken away.

Not only does Enoch represent a perfect picture of what we can expect when Jesus comes back, but Jude makes a highly significant comment about him. He specifies that Enoch was "the seventh from Adam" (Jude 14). Now that is interesting. The one person in the Bible who so accurately reflects what will occur in the millennial reign is given the designation as the seventh from Adam. I wonder why such a detail would be important. Why did Jude put this as an aside?

Could it be that God is using Enoch to point towards what Jesus' return will look like *and* to the specific time when it will occur? Perhaps Enoch, the seventh from Adam, is meant to be a prophetic picture of the seventh millennium, which confirms the timeline. At the very least, Enoch represents a relationship we can look forward to. Maybe there's more!

THE TRANSFIGURATION – A SHADOW
OF THE SECOND COMING

One of the most spectacular events that took place during Jesus' ministry was his transfiguration in front of his closest three followers: Peter, James and John. He took them up on a mountain and they witnessed how "His face shone like the sun, and his clothes became as white as light" (Matthew 17:2). The transfiguration distinctly served as a shadow of Jesus' second coming, in which He would be revealed from heaven in blazing fire in order to be glorified in His people (see 2 Thessalonians 1:7–10).

This event was "a revelation of the glory of the Son of God, a glory hidden now but to be fully revealed when He returns."[17] In other words, the disciples were getting a sneak peak of a glorified Jesus that will be revealed to the world upon His second return. I wonder if Kyle kept his secret to himself, or if he told anyone else what he did? I wonder if Kyle pulled my cousin or my brother aside and told them what was going to happen. In the transfiguration, God pulled his friends aside and secretly showed them what was in His jewelry box.

Peter understood this and linked the transfiguration to Jesus' second coming, which he explained in his letter:

We did not follow cleverly invented stories when we told you about the power *and coming* of our Lord Jesus Christ, but we *were eyewitnesses of his majesty.* For he received honor and glory from God the Father when the voice came to him from the Majestic Glory saying, "This is my Son, whom I love; with him I am well pleased." We ourselves heard this voice that came from heaven when we were with him on the sacred mountain. (2 Peter 1:16–18)

---

17   *NIV Study Bible.* (Grand Rapids, Michigan: Zondervan, 2002),

In his second letter, Peter made several references to Jesus' second coming, and he clearly saw the transfiguration as an event that was a foreshadowing of Jesus' return. What is amazing is the timing that both Matthew and Mark note as to *when* this happened. They both wrote that Jesus was transfigured "after six days" (Matthew 17:1; Mark 9:2).

This timing hardly seems coincidental. The Sabbath, or seventh day, according to Paul, was a shadow that points to Jesus. The transfiguration, which Peter pointed to as a shadow of the second coming, happened after six days. And Enoch, the person who most embodied the coming Millennial Kingdom with Jesus, was the seventh from Adam. Considering that we are approximately six thousand years from Adam and biblical prophecy suggests that Jesus will be returning soon, a seven-thousand-year timeline capped off with a millennial kingdom seems increasingly possible.

Such a possibility allows us to investigate God's Word for other treasures, and as we do so, my hope is that the following discoveries will make us fall even deeper in love with God, who is both the beginning and the end (Revelation 1:8).

Chapter Nine
The Seventh Day

As we saw in the last chapter, certain shadows of the millennial kingdom (the Sabbath and the transfiguration) fell on the seventh day. In looking more closely at Scripture, the seventh day, year, decade or century continuously points to a reality that will find its ultimate fulfillment in the second coming and potentially the seventh millennium. It is amazing to see how God weaves this pattern in His Word. The number seven is embedded throughout Scripture, and I believe it is because Jesus' return will coincide with the seventh millennium.

MOSES ON MOUNT SINAI

When Moses goes up Mount Sinai the second time, God confirms His covenant with him and appears to Moses on the seventh day:

When Moses went up on the mountain, the cloud covered it, and the glory of the Lord settled on Mount Sinai. For six days the cloud covered the mountain, and on the seventh day the Lord called to Moses from within the cloud. To the Israelites the glory of the Lord looked like a consuming fire on top of the mountain. Then Moses entered the cloud as he went on up the mountain. And he stayed on the mountain forty days and forty nights. (Exodus 24:15–18)

On the seventh day, God spoke to Moses from within a cloud. What's interesting is that when Jesus returns, he will do so on a cloud. In the book of Acts, we see that Jesus was taken from the disciples and a cloud hid Him from their sight. The disciples were looking up into the sky when two "men" spoke to them and said that Jesus was now in heaven, but He would come back the same way they saw Him go up (Acts 1:10–11). In other words, He'll emerge from the clouds.

In Luke's gospel, Jesus confirms that He'll return "coming in a cloud with power and great glory" (Luke 21:27). In John's vision, Jesus returns with the clouds, and every eye will see Him (Revelation 1:7).

God's appearance to Moses from the cloud is a prophetic picture of how Jesus will return. Moses then enters the cloud and goes into the presence of God. This is what will happen to us when Jesus returns: "For the Lord himself will come down from heaven, with a loud command, with the voice of the archangel, and with the trumpet call of God, and the dead in Christ will rise first. After that, we who are still alive and are left will be caught up together with them in the clouds to meet the Lord in the air. And so we will be with the Lord forever" (1 Thessalonians 4:16–17). Like Moses, we'll meet the Lord in the clouds when the Rapture takes place, which hypothetically would usher in the Millennial Kingdom.

THE PRIESTS AND ALTAR WERE TO BE CONSECRATED FOR SEVEN DAYS. (EX. 29)

To consecrate something is to make it holy in order to use it for a designated purpose. We are destined to live eternally with God, and we are part of His priesthood. Those who reign with

Christ when He returns will be fully consecrated in His presence: "Blessed and holy are those who have part in the first resurrection. The second death has no power over them, but they will be priests of God and of Christ and will reign with him for a thousand years" (Rev. 20:6). Just as with the priests of the Old Testament, the timeline of mankind is one whereby we are being prepared to be in God's presence. They had to be consecrated for seven days. I wonder if we are to be consecrated over seven millennia in order to dwell eternally with our Father.

EVERY SEVEN YEARS

There are certain ordinances the Israelites were to observe every seven years. As a result, the seventh year was very different from the previous six years. It resembled life before the curse (Eden) and it prefigures life in the Millennial Kingdom.

First of all, the Israelites were not allowed to plant crops in the seventh year (Lev. 25:3–4, 20–21). This was called the Sabbath year: "But in the seventh year the land is to have a Sabbath of rest, a Sabbath to the Lord" (Leviticus 25:4). It is interesting that God ordained a Sabbath year for the land. I believe God kept the Israelites from working in the seventh year to provide another shadow to the millennial kingdom. Labor was a result of the fall of man (Genesis 3:17–19), and is part of the curse of the earth. In Eden, Adam and Eve did not need to work to produce food. During the Sabbath year, the people were to eat only what the land produced by itself or *without human effort.* In the millennial kingdom, earth will be restored to an Eden-like existence. As a result, planting will not be necessary. So it was that no crops were planted in the seventh year.

Debts were cancelled and slaves set free after seven years under the Old Covenant (Deut. 15:1, 12). While many of us may need a literal cancelling of debt, the greatest bondage we have is our sin. John puts it this way: "Everyone who sins is a slave to sin" (John 8:34). When Jesus returns in the seventh millennium, there will be no more sin and our slavery to it will be broken forever. The cancelling of debts and slavery every seven years prefigured what life in the Millennial Kingdom will be like once we are no longer under the bondage of Adam's fall.

THE JUBILEE YEAR

After seven Sabbaths of years, the Israelites were commanded to celebrate a Jubilee year. This took place in the fiftieth year, or after seven times seven years (Lev. 25:8–55). Can you see how important the number seven is in God's word? The people were not allowed to work during this year and they were also to return to their family's property. If they had to sell land at any time during the previous forty-nine years, they were given their family property back during the Year of Jubilee. This was to be taken into account when land was sold. For example, if a property was sold with only three years to go before the Year of Jubilee it would be sold for a small price, since the seller would receive it back in three years.

God promised to bless the Israelites so much during the Year of Jubilee that what they harvested in the sixth year would last for three years. This celebratory year was marked by the cancellation of debts and freeing of slave and is similar to the "jubilee" we can expect when Jesus does the same in the Millennial Kingdom.

THE BABYLONIAN CAPTIVITY

One of the worst things that happened to the Jews was their captivity by the Babylonians. Their country was ravaged and desolated, and a remnant was taken into forced exile. This was the backdrop to the story of Daniel, in which he and his friends were deported to Babylon by Nebuchadnezzar. In the midst of their deportation, Daniel discovered an interesting prophecy. He found in the Scriptures where Jeremiah prophesied that Israel would be desolated for seventy years: "This is what the Lord says: 'When seventy years are completed for Babylon, I will come to you and fulfill my gracious promise to bring you back to this place'" (Jeremiah 29:10). Following this prophecy is the well-known verse in which God says He knows the plans He has for us, plans to prosper us and to bring us a hope and a future (Jeremiah 29:11).

Picture this: God's people are taken captive by the enemy. God prophesied long before it ever happened that this will only be for seven decades, and then the people will get to go home where they will prosper and have a good hope and a good future. I'm pretty sure this terrible season for Israel still has value for us today.

Like Israel, we have been taken captive by an enemy. Creation has been ravaged by sin, and the children of God are considered aliens and strangers on this planet (1 Peter 2:11). Still, this is only a temporary captivity. I believe God has given us a prophetic insight like He gave Daniel, that this state of existence will only last for seven millennia before we are restored to our permanent home… heaven.

NOAH'S SEVENTH CENTURY

Noah's life offers a prophetic timeline consistent with seven thousand years. Noah was exactly six hundred years old when the flood came upon the earth (Genesis 7:7). The purpose of the flood was to cleanse the earth and restore God's plans for humankind with a "new earth." Noah spent six centuries in a world that had become increasingly wicked (Genesis 6:5), and at the *exact* beginning of his *seventh* century, God restored and cleansed the earth. Similarly, the earth will be healed and restored with the second coming, which I expect to coincide with the exact beginning of the seventh millennium. As with the flood, the return of

Jesus will culminate in a "new earth."

There are several other interesting things about Noah. When God commanded Noah to go into the boat, He said he would send the rain "seven days from now" (Genesis 7:4). Why would God do that? Why not say, "Noah, it's time to get in the boat. It's going to start raining tomorrow."? This detail seems to strengthen the connection between Noah and Jesus' return in the seventh millennium.

Finally, Jesus himself uses Noah's life to caution the people of His return, saying:

> "No one knows about that day or hour, not even the angels in heaven, nor the Son, but only the Father. As it was in the days of Noah, so it will be at the coming of the Son of Man. For in the days before the flood, people were eating and drinking, marrying and giving in marriage, up to the day Noah entered the ark; and they knew nothing about what would happen until the flood came and took them away. That is how it will be at the coming of the Son of Man." (Matthew 24:36–39)

Jesus' point is that Noah foreshadows the second coming. Just like people were unaware of the flood, so people will not be aware of the second coming. Clearly, the situation during the time of Noah mirrors the return of Jesus. In both cases, God's plan is to restore the earth. Also, in both instances people will be unprepared. Could it be that the timing of the flood on the *seventh* day and at the beginning of Noah's *seventh* century is foreshadowing the *seventh* millennium?

ELIJAH AND THE RAIN CLOUD

Speaking of rain, Elijah played a key role in starting and ending a drought in Israel. God said it would only rain at Elijah's command. As a result, Israel was in drought for three and a half years until the moment Elijah said otherwise. Notice when God tells Elijah the drought will end: "After a long time, in the *third year*, the word of the Lord came to Elijah: 'Go and present yourself to Ahab, and I will send rain'" (1 Kings 18:1). We're going to see in the next chapter how the third day from Jesus is the same as the seventh day from Adam. The third day perfectly parallels the seventh day, and the numbers seven and three have the same scriptural meaning.

Something interesting happens when Elijah finally does speak an end to the drought. He tells Ahab (the king) that he hears the sound of "heavy rain" (1 Kings 18:41). Elijah says this even though there is not a cloud in the sky. He then tells his servant to go and look toward the sea. The servant does this but he does not see anything. Seven times Elijah instructs him to go back. On the seventh trip, the servant sees a small cloud the size of a man's fist. Immediately, the sky grew black, the wind rose and there was a heavy rain (1 Kings 18:41–45). Surely, it is significant that the rain cloud only appeared on the seventh time, and the rain came in the third year!

There are those who link Jesus' return to the latter rain (which we'll address more in chapter 11). They link the first coming to the former rain and the spring feasts (chapter 11), and the second coming to the latter rain and the unfulfilled spring feasts (chapter 12). The story of Elijah is probably the most significant story in Scripture regarding a heavy rain (other than the flood account). I do not think the timing is coincidental. I think God is drawing our attention to the timing of the latter rain, which is linked to Jesus' return.

GOD COUNTED TIME IN SEVENS WITH THE FIRST COMING

This theory can be further supported in part by the fact that there is biblical precedent for God to measure time in "sevens."

The coming of Jesus is actually anticipated by seventy sevens (Dan. 9:25–27).

One of the more controversial and intriguing prophetic scriptures is the seventy "sevens" found in Daniel 9. Here, God gives a timeline for the coming of Jesus, which will achieve the following six purposes: "to finish transgression, to put an end to sin, to atone for wickedness, to bring in everlasting righteousness, to seal up vision and prophesy and to anoint the most holy" (Daniel 9:24). Jesus clearly fulfills this prophesy and the timeline of sevens that was given in anticipation of His coming.

The seventy sevens are broken up into three groups, which further emphasize God's use of the numbers seven and three as a prophetic timepiece. The timeline is grouped as follows:

- Period One – seven sevens
- Period Two – sixty-two sevens
- Period Three – one seven (Daniel 9:25–27)

The exact time frames these periods represent is disputed, but it is generally accepted that the seventy sevens represents seventy periods of seven years (490 years), which culminate in Jesus' first coming.

If Jesus' first coming was accurately predicted based on a timeline measured by sevens, it is certainly feasible that God would use a timeline measured in seven years/millennia to anticipate the second coming of Jesus. Furthermore, the prophecies mentioned above are partly fulfilled in the first coming and ultimately fulfilled in the second coming. For this reason, it would be acceptable to apply the seventy sevens to measure time before both Jesus' first and second coming, which is what Isaac Newton did to predict the return of Christ between 2000 and 2050 AD.

We'll look at this more closely in Chapter 11, which explores the remarkable way Daniel 9 could predict the second coming.

Chapter Ten
The Third Day

The number seven is not the only important number that God uses. One of the more significant biblical shadows is that of the third day. This is what the band "Third Day" draws its name from.[18] A study of Scripture reveals that God shows up on the third day. The most well-known example of this is the resurrection of Jesus on the third day, but there are many more. In order to appreciate this scriptural shadow in the context of seven thousand years, we need to understand that there are two ways to count time.

TWO HISTORICAL STARTING POINTS

The first way to count time is the one that has been discussed thus far in the book. We can count from "the beginning" – from Adam. The second way is the one people currently use, and that is to count time from the birth of Christ. Biblically, Jesus is referred to as a second Adam – or a second starting point: "The first man was from the dust of the earth, the second man from heaven" (1 Corinthians 15:47).

Adam is actually referred to as a pattern of the one to come

---

18   http://www.thirdday.com/news?n_id=320

– Jesus (Romans 5:14). The pattern that Adam starts is that he would eternally impact those who came after him. Jesus completes the pattern set forth by Adam, by bringing eternal life to those who are born of Him. As the second and *last* Adam (1 Corinthians 15:45), Jesus serves as a starting point for human history.

If we use the second method to count time, then the third millennium from Christ is the same as the seventh millennium from Adam. The two are one in the same. Just as Jesus rose from the dead on the third day, the seven thousand year timeline anticipates He will return in the third millennium from his death, or the third day.

The numbers three and seven have the same biblical meaning. They are both numbers of perfection and completion.

Another interesting link between them is found in the Old Testament cleansing regulations. When people became unclean, they were commanded by God to purify themselves on the <u>third</u> and on the <u>seventh</u> day (Numbers 19:12). I believe God links these two days in the purification because they are one and the same day, and because purification will happen in the Millennial Kingdom. This is a profound parallel.

These numbers are also linked when Moses goes up Mount Sinai the first and second time. On the first trip, God spoke to Moses on the third day, and the second time He spoke to Moses on the seventh day (Exodus 19:16–19; 24:15–18).

Since the third day from Jesus is the same as the seventh day from Adam, we can also look at the use of the third day in Scripture to anticipate Jesus' return. We find that when we examine these references, they fit perfectly with a seven-thousand-year timeline.

THE SIGN OF JONAH

Jesus tells his listeners that the only "sign" given to their generation would be the sign of Jonah: "A wicked and adulterous generation asks for a miraculous sign! But none will be given it except the sign of the prophet Jonah. For as Jonah was three days and three nights in the belly of a huge fish, so the Son of Man will be three days and three nights in the heart of the earth" (Luke 11:29).

We cannot dispute that the sign of Jesus' generation was that of the third day. We need to understand that God purposed Jonah's time in the belly of the whale. God intentionally kept Jonah there for three days so he could establish a shadow that would later find its fulfillment in Christ. His timing is deliberate. We should be able to agree on this much at least.

In studying biblical prophecy, a very interesting truth emerges. Prophecy does not always relate to a single future event. It can actually find fulfillment in multiple events. "The Hebrew idea of prophecy is a pattern that is repeated, multiple fulfillments with one ultimate fulfillment. Each of the multiple fulfillments is both a type of, and a lesson on, the ultimate fulfillment."[19]

The ultimate fulfillment of the sign of Jonah could very well be the second coming of Christ, not the first. If so, the sign of Jonah is also a sign for our generation – the one which will not pass away before the return of Christ. Just as Jesus and Jonah spent two days "buried," so Jesus will spend two thousand years away before He returns for a third millennium of peace and restoration on earth. We should keep in mind that with the Lord a day is like a thousand years, and a thousand years is like a day.

THIRD DAY EXAMPLES

It is actually exciting to see the other examples of God coming on the third day. This pattern gives incredible weight to the idea that Jesus could return on the third day (millennium) after His Resurrection.

---

19 http://www.inplainsite.org/html/old_testament_prophecy.html.

1. ABRAHAM ON MOUNT MORIAH (GENESIS 22)

In this story, Abraham symbolized God, and Isaac symbolized Jesus. God asked Abraham to take "your *only* son, Isaac, whom you love" and sacrifice him (Genesis 22:2). Three times God intentionally refers to Isaac as Abraham's only son (Genesis 22:2, 12, 16). He is doing this to draw our attention to what it meant for him to send Jesus: "For God so loved the world, that He gave his *only* son ..." (John 3:16). God was willing to give His only son, and this test proved that Abraham would be willing to do the same. When events like this happen three times, they are meant to get our attention as something God wants to emphasize. Similar examples are when Samuel went to Eli three times after hearing God, and Jesus asked Peter three times whether he loved Him.

When Abraham got to the place where he was to sacrifice Isaac, he found a ram in the bush, which foreshadowed the first coming of Jesus. All of this happened on the third day, which foreshadows the timing of the second coming!

2. MOUNT SINAI (EXODUS 19:10–18)

When the Israelites arrived at Mount Sinai, God gave them specific instructions to consecrate themselves for two days because He was going to come on the third day. For two days, the Israelites prepared themselves for the arrival of God. The church is currently in a season of sanctification in preparation for Jesus' return. The good news is that what the Israelites were commanded to physically do, Jesus has done for us with His sacrifice on the cross. We are made clean and given garments of righteousness when we believe in Him.

On the third day, God arrives on Mount Sinai with the sound of a very loud trumpet. As we will see, this is very significant because Jesus will also return at the sound of a trumpet (Matthew

24:30–31). The trumpet blast links this appearance of God with the second coming of Jesus, thus giving us reason to also link the timing of these events.

3. THE ISRAELITES ENTER THE PROMISED LAND (JOSHUA 1)

When Joshua takes over command of the Israelites, he gives the people the following message: "Get your supplies ready. Three days from now you will cross the Jordan here to go in and take possession of the land the Lord your God is giving you for your own" (Joshua 1:11).

Again the people are commanded to ready themselves for two days. On the third day, they are told they will possess the Promised Land. This represents the eternal inheritance in the Lord we will fully possess with the second coming of Christ.

4. HEZEKIAH'S HEALING (2 KINGS 20:5–8)

When Hezekiah becomes deathly ill, God promises to heal him on the third day. As with Jonah, this timing is deliberate. Our physical, spiritual and emotional healing is initially fulfilled when Jesus rose from the dead on the third day and defeated death. But our healing finds its ultimate fulfillment in Jesus' second return, which I believe will occur on the third day (millennium) after Jesus' resurrection. This period will usher in a thousand year reign and an ensuing eternity where there will be no sickness or death (Revelation 21:4).

5. ESTHER APPEARS BEFORE KING XERXES ON THE THIRD DAY (ESTHER 5:1–2)

This is highly significant on a number of levels. The Jewish nation was under threat of annihilation. Their one hope was that Esther, the queen, was a Jew. The idea was that she should risk her life to appear unsummoned before the king and plead for her people. Esther asked the people to fast for three days before she presented herself to the king. She then put on her royal robes and appealed to King Xerxes for his favor <u>on the third day</u>.

Esther represents a new covenant believer. Because of the sacrifice of Jesus, we too have royal robes to wear (Galatians 3:27; Isaiah 61:10). Furthermore, we are the bride of Christ (Ephesians 5:27), just as Esther was the bride of the king. On the third day, Esther's identity allowed her to find favor with the king, and her people were saved. This same favor and salvation will be given to those in Christ when Jesus returns.

The period of fasting before the third day could well represent the period we are currently in. When Jesus' disciples were criticized for not fasting, He replies,

"Can you make the guests of the bridegroom fast while he is with them? But the time will come when the bridegroom will be taken from them; in those days they will fast." (Luke 5:34–35)

Notice the wedding language. Jesus is clearly the bridegroom, and we are His guests. He tells us there will be fasting when He's taken away. When He returns to His bride (us), the fasting will end. Could the timing of our "fasting" be linked to that in the book of Esther? If so, we can anticipate that, like Esther, we, the Bride, will enter the presence of Jesus, the bridegroom, on the third day/millennium.

What makes this shadow significant is that it can only be fulfilled on the "third day" following Jesus' death. Our royal robes were only provided by His death and resurrection, and our time of fasting only began with Jesus' death!

6. A PROPHETIC DECLARATION (HOSEA 6:2)

After two days he will revive us; on the third day he will restore us, that we may live in his presence.

This verse provides a profound prophetic declaration. God promises to revive us and restore us on the third day so we can live in his presence. In the millennium, we will dwell fully in the presence of God, and Hosea links this to the third day. What is interesting about this verse as a prophetic declaration is that it was only partially fulfilled (at best) with the Resurrection of Jesus. It will be completely fulfilled when Jesus returns, at which point we will be living fully in His presence.

7. WEDDING AT CANA (JOHN 2:1–2)

On the third day a wedding took place at Cana in Galilee. Jesus' mother was there, and Jesus and his disciples had also been invited to the wedding.

As with many other events, it is striking that the timing of this is not further explained. The third day from what? John does not elaborate beyond telling us the wedding was on the third day. This is definitely significant. Details such as this are given to us for a reason.

As we have already seen, the imagery used surrounding the return of Christ is strongly linked to a wedding between Him and us. An entire book could be written just on wedding language in the Bible. Nevertheless, the one recorded wedding that Jesus attended happened *on the third day*. The theory of this book is that Jesus will return in the third millennium from his death in order to consummate His relationship with us, His bride.

I do not believe these events are mere coincidence. Details are incredibly important in the Bible. I will concede, however, that we cannot manipulate them into supporting whatever we would like. For that reason, I want to emphasize this is only a theory, and it will be tested with time. That being said, the examples of the third day in the Scripture lend incredible weight to the possibility that Jesus could return in the third millennium from His resurrection or the seventh millennium from Adam.

Chapter Eleven
Daniel's Seventy 'Sevens'

The ninth chapter of Daniel gives a timeline for the coming of the Messiah based on seventy 'sevens' or four hundred and ninety years. We have already seen that this was fulfilled once in the first coming, but this chapter examines how this is also a prophecy regarding the second coming of Jesus. What we find is deserving of our attention. The information found in this chapter may give us the most specific timeframe for the second coming, and amazingly it affirms the theory presented in this book.

Jesus actually linked Daniel's seventy 'sevens' to His **second** coming. In outlining a series of end-time events in Matthew 24, Jesus referenced Daniel's prophecy. He says, "So when you see standing in the holy place 'the abomination that causes desolation' spoken of through the prophet Daniel - let the reader understand - then let those who are in Judea flee to the mountains" (Matthew 24:15-16).

This is critical on a number of levels. Let's look closely at the passage in Daniel Jesus was referring to:

Seventy 'sevens' are decreed for your people and your holy city to finish transgression, to put an end to sin, to atone for wickedness, to bring in everlasting righteousness, to seal up vision and prophecy and to anoint the most holy.

Know and understand this: From the issuing of the decree to restore and rebuild Jerusalem until the Anointed One, the ruler, comes, there will be seven 'sevens,' and sixty-two 'sevens.' It will be rebuilt with streets and a trench, but in times of trouble. After the sixty-two 'sevens', the Anointed One will be cut off and will have nothing. The people of the ruler who will come will destroy the city and the sanctuary. The end will come like a flood: War will continue until the end, and desolations have been decreed. He will confirm a covenant with many for one 'seven.' In the middle of the 'seven' he will put an end to sacrifice and offering. And on a wing of temple he will set up an abomination that causes desolation, until the end that is decreed is poured out on him (Daniel 9:24-27).

We've seen that this passage has been used to accurately predict the first coming of Jesus by counting seventy 'sevens' from the time of Ezra and Nehemiah. But this is NOT what Jesus is saying in Matthew 24. Jesus is saying that Daniel's prophecy will be fulfilled in the second coming. How is it that the church has missed this key detail?

Not only does Jesus mention this, but there are other reasons why these verses indicate the second coming. First of all, the passage describes the end. It says things like, "**the end** will come like a flood"; "War will continue until **the end**" and the abomination that causes desolation will be set up "until **the end**." There is also a case to made that the final three events in 9:23 will only be finalized with the second coming: bringing in everlasting righteousness, sealing up vision and prophecy, and anointing the most holy. In other words, Jesus clearly fulfilled the first part of that passage in His first coming, and will fulfill the second part when He returns. Finally the other events of Daniel 9 are also mentioned by Jesus as end-time events: wars, desolations and the destruction of Jerusalem.

Jesus specifically mentioned the abomination that causes desolation, which Daniel said will be set up in the temple in the middle of the last seven. Daniel outlined the sequence of events as follows:

1) A decree will be issued to rebuild and restore Jerusalem (9:25).
2) Seven 'sevens' and sixty 'sevens' (483 years) will pass until the Anointed One will be cut off.'
3) Jerusalem will be destroyed.
4) Wars will continue as well as desolations.
5) He (the anti-Christ) will confirm a covenant for one 'seven.'
6) In the middle of the 'seven' the anti-Christ will set up an abomination that causes desolation.

The last seven refers to a final seven year tribulation period with the revealing of the anti-Christ at the midpoint. In all of this, a key detail stood out to me. There is a starting point to these 490 years! I was shocked that this had not been mentioned in mainstream prophetic writings to this point. The church has been so consumed with applying the 490 years to Jesus' first coming that it did not consider the obvious application that Jesus mentions. Perhaps our eyes have been blinded for a time such as this. God may have been saving this in His jewelry box.

Daniel writes that the seventy sevens will **begin** with a decree to rebuild Jerusalem. He says, "From the issuing of the decree to restore and rebuild Jerusalem until the Anointed One, the ruler, comes, there will be seven 'sevens,' and sixty-two 'sevens' " (9:25). We have a starting point to this prophecy. This excited me, so I took the year 2028 and subtracted 490 from it and Googled whether Jerusalem was rebuilt in 1538. I nearly fell out of my chair when I found out it was. You can't make this stuff up. This discovery has been THE MOST SOBERING insight that I have gained on this topic.

Rebuilding these walls was not just a casual event that happened every few decades. This building process took years. A project of this scale had only happened once before and that was during Nehemiah's time. This is not a coincidental detail. We need to understand that Bible scholars used the first rebuilding of the walls to predict Jesus' first coming and that it is reasonable to do the same regarding the second coming...even more so given Jesus' acknowledgement of Daniel's prophecy and the end times.

When this happened, an Ottoman King, Suleiman I, ordered the walls to be rebuilt around 1535, and they were constructed somewhere between 1537-1541.[20] This supports the theory of this book. Archaeological evidence exists of this decree[21], but there is some ambiguity about the exact timing of the decree. It was made somewhere between 1535 and 1538. [22] If we add sixty-nine sevens, or 483 years, to those dates we get a date range of 2018 - 2021 for the sixty-nine sevens to end. This is important because the final seven year tribulation would ensue. This would potentially put the second coming between 2025 and 2028 should the final 'seven' begin immediately after the sixty-nine 'sevens.' This fits the 7000 year timeline.

If this prophecy is referring to Suleiman, then the timing of his decree is very significant. Barry Setterfield researched this and looked for the earliest evidence of a decree given by King Suleiman. The first record he could find was inscribed on the fountain at the Jaffa Gate. It said Suleiman ordered the construction of that fountain on June 29, 1536[23]. Adding 483 years to that

---

20 https://en.wikipedia.org/wiki/Walls_of_Jerusalem

21 http://museum.imj.org.il/imagine/galleries/viewItemE.
    asp?case=7&itemNum=374383

22 http://midseventiethweekrapture.blogspot.com/2015/02/suleiman-and-
    70-weeks-of-daniel.html

23 http://www.setterfield.org/jerusalem_wall.html

date takes us to June 29, 2019. While I don't think we can or should be that specific, we need to be aware that we could see the 483 years come to an end around that time. According to Setterfield, it's unknown whether the command to rebuild the walls came before or after this. Given that the first wall was built in 1537, it seems reasonable to narrow down the end of the 483 years to between 2018 and 2020.

What will happen after the 483 years? Daniel says the Anointed One will be cut off, and the people of the ruler (anti-Christ) will destroy Jerusalem. Based on Daniel's prophecy, there is good reason to conclude that Jerusalem will be attacked at the end of the 483 years, and the final tribulation will be triggered. It is incredible that this could potentially happen any time over the next couple of years. While I'm not 100% sure that events will unfold in this way, the language here merits our attention.

It is also worth noting what motivated this Muslim sultan to rebuild Jerusalem. This was a highly unusual event. King Suleiman had a series of dreams in which lions were chasing him. When he finally stopped and asked the lions what he needed to do to be spared, he was given the following instructions:

*"... the Prophet appeared to him in a 'blessed night' and told him: 'Oh, Sulaiman, you will have the rulership for forty-six years and will make many conquests. Your offspring will not die out to the end of time. My kindness will always extend to you. You **should spend these spoils** on embellishing Mecca and Medina, and **for the fortification of the citadel of Jerusalem,** in order to repulse the unbelievers, when they attempt to take possession of Jerusalem during the reigns of your followers. **You should also embellish its sanctuary with water basins** and offer annual money gifts to the Dervishes there, and also embellish the Rock of Allah **and rebuild Jerusalem.'** Such being the order of the Prophet, Sulaiman Khan rose at once from his sleep and sent from his*

spoils one thousand purses to Medina and another thousand purses to Jerusalem (Auld and Hillenbrand 2000 p.353)."[24]

This is amazing. Daniel's prophecy stated that Jerusalem would be "rebuilt with streets and a trench, but in times of trouble." In this dream, King Suleiman was instructed to embellish the sanctuary with water basins. In fact, he rebuilt the fountains before ever working on the walls.[25] Remarkably, this also happened during troubled times, as King Suleiman was engaged in the Ottoman-Safavid War.[26]

This is profound on so many levels. King Suleiman didn't even serve God, but it would seem God prompted him to rebuild the walls in a dream in order to set up a countdown to the end times.

I know this can be overwhelming, but there are few indicators to look out for. Remember to treat this like the Magi treated the star. The Magi were aware of the possibility of a star and kept an eye out for its fulfillment. With that in mind, what should we watch for? First of all, if this application is correct, the 483 years will culminate with Jerusalem being attacked. Should we witness that event, then we need to understand it is only a matter of time before Jesus returns. The text in Daniel could allow for a period of time between when Jerusalem is attacked and when a peace treaty is proposed. Nevertheless, once Jerusalem is attacked, we will see end-time events escalate quickly, as "the end will come like a flood." There will be wars, earthquakes and famines. When a covenant or peace treaty is initiated the Tribulation will have begun and we will have seven years before the end. A serious attack on Jerusalem and subsequent treaty will mark a key and final transition for us.

Natural disasters, wars and pestilences will permanently change life for us. At this point, Christians need to be prepared.

---

24 http://www.setterfield.org/jerusalem_wall.html
25 http://www.setterfield.org/jerusalem_wall.html
26 http://www.setterfield.org/jerusalem_wall.html

We are warned of famines, and we are warned of not being able to buy food if we don't have the mark of the beast (Rev 13:17). We should be ready for this. If we can anticipate these things based on Scripture, we can position ourselves to help others and to point out the accuracy of God's word. This could even allow for some incredible ministry opportunities, especially if these events do not take us by surprise.

I am afraid that much of the church has been lulled to sleep regarding this topic because of our rapture mindset. If we believe we will not be here, then we will not even consider what to do if we are. The next chapter looks at the rapture and whether it is reasonable to conclude that Christians will be raptured before the final seven year tribulation.

Chapter Twelve
What About the Rapture?

When I initially published this book, I did not cover the rapture. I had some strong opinions but not enough knowledge to confidently enter the discussion in a meaningful way. Since that time, I am convinced it is necessary to discuss this. I feel the church has largely ignored Scripture regarding the rapture and adopted the tradition of man. While this really does not matter in terms of our salvation, it needs to be considered in the context of this book. If we are reaching the rapidly approaching culmination of the ages, then we need to understand how the rapture will apply to us.

As with the rest of this book, there is room for us to disagree on these matters and still walk together as brothers and sisters in Christ. I joked with our church when I taught on the rapture, "If I'm wrong about this, you can go up first...in front of me." My point was simple: in the grand scheme of our eternal salvation, this is a relatively minor issue. We'll all get to go up if we have accepted Jesus Christ as our Lord and Savior, irrespective of when that event takes place.

My personal understanding of the rapture was formed by reading the "Left Behind" series. I was probably not even a Christian when I read those books, but they contributed greatly to my hunger for God and to my ultimate surrender to Him. To that end, I am forever thankful for Tim Lahaye and Jerry Jenkins.

It was also their book "Are We Living in the End Times" that God used initially to confirm this 7,000 years theory. Still, as I studied Scripture for myself, I had a hard time reconciling the timing of the rapture in those books with what the Bible said.

The word "rapture" is not mentioned in the Bible, but neither is the word "trinity" so this doesn't need to bother us. The concept is sound. Believers will definitely be "raptured" or "taken up" to meet Jesus. Perhaps this is most descriptively seen in 1 Thessalonians 5:16-17,

> For the Lord himself will come down from heaven, with a loud command, with the voice of the archangel and with the trumpet call of God, and the dead in Christ will rise first. After that, we who are still alive and are left **will be caught up together with them in the clouds to meet the Lord in the air.** And so we will be with the Lord forever.

As with everything in this book, timing is what matters. The debate over the rapture is really about when it will occur. There are three general ideas here, and I've used their abbreviated form: pre-trib, mid-trib and post trib. The theories are:

Pre-Trib: the church will be raptured before the tribulation (Daniel's final seven).

Mid-Trib: the church will be raptured during the tribulation.

Post-Trib: the church will be raptured at the end of the tribulation.

The "Left Behind" series was based on a pre-trib rapture. If a pre-trib rapture is incorrect and a large portion of the church is banking on this "get out of jail free" card, they are not going to be ready for what is to come.

Before we look into Scripture, it is worth noting that the pre-trib rapture is a relatively new concept in the body of Christ, emerging only in the 1830's.[27] It is also largely American, meaning many parts of the world don't ascribe to this theology. I believe that much of the church has blindly accepted this theology simply because it was what we were taught and because it makes us feel good not to have to think about the tribulation. I was certainly in that camp, but the more I studied Scripture the harder it was for me to hold that position.

WHAT DID JESUS SAY?

We need to examine the passage in 1 Thessalonians 5:16-17 in light of what Jesus said. Jesus addressed the end times in Matthew, Mark and Luke. In doing so, Jesus warned us of what would happen in the end after Jerusalem is attacked and after the abomination that causes desolation is revealed. Jesus never told us that His people will not face those events. Surely, if there were to be a pre-trib rapture, we could expect Jesus to say something along the lines of, "Hey, some bad things are going to happen, but you do not have to worry about them because you will not be here." Jesus did the opposite. He emphasized the need to look for the signs and to be prepared for what is to come.

Let's look at Matthew 24:27-31 to help bring clarity to this

For as the lightning that comes from the east is visible even in the west, so will be the coming of the Son of Man. Wherever there is a carcass, there the vultures will gather. **Immediately after the distress** of those days, 'the sun will be darkened, and the moon will not give its light; the

---

27 http://www.bible.ca/rapture-origin-john-nelson-darby-1830ad.htm

stars will fall from the sky, and the heavenly bodies will be shaken.' **At that time** the sign of the Son of Man will appear in the sky, and all the nations of the earth will mourn. They will see the Son of Man coming on the clouds of the sky, with power and great glory. And he will send his angels with a loud trumpet call, and they will gather his elect from the four winds, from one end of the heavens to the other.

This is a loaded passage of Scripture with several points we need to consider. First, there are many parallels with the passage in 1 Thessalonians 5:16-17.

We see the following events in BOTH passages:

- Jesus comes down from heaven.
- Jesus is in the clouds.
- There is a trumpet blast.
- Angels are present both times.
- The elect are "caught up" in Thessalonians 5 and "gathered from the winds" in Matthew 24.

While there are some who may try to distinguish these as two separate events, I cannot but conclude that these passages are describing the same thing. Matthew 24:31 would also seem to indicate a rapture, as it says the angels "will gather his elect from the four winds, from one end of the heavens to the other." From this, I think it is safe to conclude that Matthew 24 is just as much a rapture reference as any other.

Second, when Jesus returns the entire world will know it. Matthew 24:27 says that "as lightning that comes from the east is visible in the west, so will be the coming of the Son of Man." Jesus is saying that in the same way we can see lightning in the clouds from a distance, all people will be able to see Him when

He comes "on the clouds of the sky." He is responding to the false reports that will go out among many saying, "The Messiah is here or there." We will not need anyone to tell us when Jesus comes back. Nor will we need to go anywhere to find him. He will be supernaturally visible to all people at the same time. The book of Revelation confirms this saying, "Look, he is coming with the clouds, and every eye will see him" (1:7). What a moment that will be.

Now consider the rapture passage of 1 Thessalonians 4:16-17 " For the Lord himself will come down from heaven, with a loud command, with the voice of the archangel and with the trumpet call of God, and the dead in Christ will rise first. After that, we who are still alive and are left will be caught up together with them in the clouds to meet the Lord in the air. And so we will be with the Lord forever ." Is this to be some secret event as envisioned by the pre-trib teaching? Of course not! Jesus is not going to come secretly on the clouds with angels and a trumpet in one instance, and later come unmistakably on the clouds with angels and a trumpet in another. In assuming that Matthew 24 and 1 Thessalonians 5 are describing the same event, we can conclude that when a rapture event happens, it will be public.

Third, Jesus tells us WHEN this will happen. He said His coming on the clouds with the angels and with the trumpet blast, will happen "immediately after the distress of those days." Jesus had just outlined everything that would take place. He warned of how great the distress would be and then He said He'll return *after* that distress. In one of the more sobering passages, He said, "For then there will be great distress, unequaled from the beginning of the world until now - and never to be equaled again. If those days had not been cut short, no one would survive, but for the sake of the elect those days will be shortened." Wow. So things will become the worst they have ever been or ever will be. After that, Jesus will return and gather His elect. He gives us a consolation here: for our sake, this distress is limited and shortened or else no one would survive. I'm not sure how we're supposed to feel about that...

People who advocate a pre-trib rapture have a serious problem with the elect in this passage and in others. They have tried to reconcile this by saying the elect represents Israel, but we don't see any significant reference supporting this. In my opinion this is an attempt to conform Scripture to fit doctrine instead of letting doctrine be formed by Scripture. Jesus never distinguished between the church and Israel here. He never said, "Hey, New Testament church, you don't have to face this. I'm just making Israel go through the great distress." With all that Jesus tells us about the end times, I'm sure He'd want to clarify this if it were the case.

Finally, the rapture follows many distresses. Before Jesus spoke about coming on the clouds with a trumpet and gathering the elect in Matthew 24, He told us all the things that are going to happen. The list is quite lengthy. Before we are ever taken up the following will take place:

- Nation will rise against nation and kingdom against kingdom. (24:7)
- There will be famines and earthquakes that are the beginnings of the birth pains. (24:7- 8).
- Christians will be persecuted and put to death and hated by nations. (24:9)
- Many will turn away from the faith and betray each other. (24:10)
- False prophets will appear and deceive many people. (24:11)
- Wickedness will increase, causing the love of most to grow cold. (24:12)
- The gospel will be preached to all nations. (24:14)
- The abomination that causes desolation will stand in the temple. (24:15)

- There will be great distress that has never been seen before, nor will ever be seen again (24:21)
- False Christs and false prophets will appear and perform great signs and miracles to deceive the elect. (24:24)
- The sun will be darkened, the moon will not give its light, the stars will fall from the sky and the heavenly bodies will be shaken. (24:29)

Did you notice that several of those points specifically refer to what will happen to believers? After all these things, Jesus said He would return "at that time" to gather the elect (Matthew 24:31).

2 THESSALONIANS' RAPTURE REFERENCE

Just in case one is tempted to think that the elect who are "gathered...from the four winds" mentioned in Matthew 24 are somehow different than the people "caught up" in 1 Thessalonians 4, let's look at another key passage. In 2 Thessalonians 2:1-3 Paul writes,

Concerning, the coming of our Lord Jesus Christ and our being gathered to him, we ask you brothers not to be easily unsettled or alarmed by some prophecy, report or letter supposed to have come from us, saying that the day of the Lord has already come. **Don't let anyone deceive you in any way, for that day will not come until the rebellion occurs and the man of lawlessness is revealed,** the man doomed to destruction. He will oppose and will exalt himself over everything that is called God or is worshipped, so **that he sets himself up in God's temple, proclaiming himself to be God.**

Paul is clearly referring to the rapture when he speaks about the coming of Jesus and our being "gathered to him." He says that this day will NOT come until the man of lawlessness is revealed and he sets himself up in God's temple. This is the abomination that causes desolation that Daniel mentioned. It is also the same event Jesus references in Matthew 24. In both passages, we find the rapture happening after this key moment. We are told specifically not to be deceived and to think that Jesus has come UNTIL this event occurs. As we've seen in Daniel 9, this will occur half way through the final seven.

THE DANGERS OF AN INCORRECT RAPTURE THEOLOGY

There are a number of problems that emerge with wrongly accepting a pre-trib rapture. The first major problem is that we won't heed Jesus' warnings. This may sound over-simplistic, but Jesus warns us for a reason. When we choose to inoculate ourselves from end times events with our own reasoning, we will be unprepared for what will come.

In Matthew 24 Jesus tells us to "keep watch" and "Be ready" (vs. 42 & 44). In Mark 13:23 when He taught about the end times, Jesus told us "So be on your guard; I have told you everything ahead of time." Jesus can't get any more plain than this. He went on to say in that chapter, "Be on guard! Be alert"... "Keep watch... "If he comes suddenly, do not let him find you sleeping." (33, 35, 36). Pre-trib thinking could cause people to overlook and/ or misapply those warnings. Instead of considering everything Jesus told us ahead of time, we can mistakenly insert the rapture in front of it all and assume we don't have to think too much about the tribulation. The very fact that Jesus speaks so much about these events should encourage us to consider them. We should not stick our heads in the sand over an issue Jesus has been this clear about.

Paul also issues a warning about what is to come. Immediately after giving us the most descriptive verse of the rapture in 1 Thessalonians 4:16-17, Paul said that the day of the Lord should not come as a surprise: "But you, brothers, are not in darkness so that this day should surprise you like a thief...let us be alert and self-controlled." (1 Thessalonians 5:4,6). Paul specifically called this the "Day of the Lord," which is synonymous with the Day of Judgment or the last day. If Paul were somehow separating that day from the rapture he just mentioned, surely he would have said so. Surely, he would have been more clear. You have to perform cartwheels with words to somehow arrive a different conclusion here.

Another consequence for people who hold to the pre-trib rapture is that they could be quickly disillusioned. Imagine thinking you will not have to face the worst distress in the history of mankind, only to find out you were wrong, your pastor was wrong and now it's too late. Ironically, the people who may be "left behind" in Daniel's final seven could be Christians themselves who are ill-equipped to deal with the very turmoil that they had been warned about.

Many believers could end up disillusioned with God, with their leaders and with God's Word. Couple that with disasters happening all around them, and an increase in wickedness, and one can begin to see how the love of most could grow cold. This is a serious problem. Instead of being ready to be the light in a dark time and point to God's sovereignty and the Truth of His Word, people could resign themselves to a lukewarm state of existence where everything they thought they knew had been upended.

Where does this leave us? We are left with a mid-trib rapture that would take place sometime after the abomination that causes desolation is revealed, or we are left with a post-trib rapture. There are reasons to consider both options. Either way, I believe that when we are taken up, it will be at the second coming of Jesus and we will meet Him in the air. Sometime after Jesus appears in the clouds, He will come to earth and finish business. He will overthrow Satan and usher in the Millennial Kingdom.

That will be a great moment for God and His church. May we be diligent and aware of the events that will lead up to this, and may the peace and faith we carry lead many others to the Lord during that time. This will be our finest hour. Let's embrace it.

Chapter Thirteen

The Seven Festivals of the Messiah – The Spring Festivals

As we've seen, the Old Testament is very prophetic in nature. God clearly wanted people to know He had a plan when Jesus came the first time. There were a number of prophecies and shadows that pointed to Jesus' first coming. Among these were the Jewish festivals God commanded the Israelites to keep on a yearly basis. These were so important that the Israelites travelled to Jerusalem three times a year in order to observe them.

At this point, we should not be surprised to learn that there were <u>seven</u> Festivals/Feasts God ordained in Leviticus 23 for His people to observe. Nor should it surprise us to learn that Jesus was meant to fulfill them. They were real events designed to fore-shadow the coming of Christ. What is incredibly profound is that four of these feasts were fulfilled in exact detail when Jesus came. Three remain unfulfilled and point to the second coming and, in the context of this work, are worthy of our full attention.

Much of the following information regarding these feasts in the next two chapters comes from Edward Chumney's book on the feasts, *The Seven Festivals of the Messiah*.

In this chapter, we will consider the four spring feasts: Passover, Unleavened Bread, First Fruits and Pentecost. These festivals were instituted when Moses delivered the Israelites from Egypt, beginning with the celebration of Passover and ending fifty days later when God appeared to Moses on Mount Sinai. These feasts were all fulfilled in the fifty days between Jesus celebrating the Passover, dying on the cross, resurrecting and sending the Holy Spirit. Each feast that originated with the Egyptian exodus is perfectly met in terms of the *timing* of Jesus' first coming.

Chumney explains this correlation in detail: "from the Exodus story, we can see that the Lamb was slain on the fourteenth of Nisan, the day of Passover. On the fifteenth of Nisan, the day of Unleavened Bread, the people left Egypt; on the seventeenth of Nisan the children of Israel crossed the Red Sea; and 50 days later on the Feast of Weeks, or Passover, God gave the Torah (instruction) on Mount Sinai."[28]

"Jesus died on Passover (Nisan 14), was in the sepulcher [grave] on the day of Unleavened Bread (Nisan 15), and was resurrected on the day of First Fruits (Nisan 17), and the Holy Spirit empowered the believers 50 days following Jesus' resurrection on the day of Pentecost."[29] Clearly, timing is significant for our God. His prophetic timing establishes patterns that anticipate the coming of Jesus.

God commanded His people to go through incredible trouble to observe these feasts because they were going to be fulfilled when Jesus came the first *and* second time. The festivals were designed by God to help people recognize the coming of Jesus. It is right for us to consider them in terms of the timing of Jesus' second coming.

---

28 Chumney, *Seven Festivals*, 15–16.
29 Ibid, 16.

We already saw in the eighth chapter how Jesus fulfilled the Passover. This was the feast meant to commemorate the moment death "passed over" the Israelite families that had applied the blood of the perfect lamb to their doorposts. Jesus was the Lamb of God who saved us from death, and He died exactly on Passover. Every detail of Jesus' death fulfilled this feast.

Chumney makes an incredible observation about Passover:

God commanded Israel to take a lamb on the 10th day of Nisan and set it aside until the fourteenth day... Eschatologically, these four days that the lamb was hidden is prophetic of the people's expectations that the Messiah would come 4,000 years from the creation of Adam as part of the seven-thousand-year plan of God to redeem both man and the earth back to how things were in the Garden of Eden. These four days are prophetic of the Messiah *Yeshua* being hid from the world and not coming to earth for four days or 4,000 years from the creation of Adam.[30]

Wow. This clearly supports the thesis of this book. Chumney affirms a seven-thousand-year timeline. He also explains the reason the lamb was kept hidden for four days was to represent the four thousand years between Adam and Jesus, which links a single day to a thousand year period of history.

He continues in this passage to say: "Linking Psalm 90:4 to each day in creation, G-d ordained each day in creation to be prophetic of a thousand years of time and the entire redemption to take seven thousand years to complete from the fall of man in the Garden of Eden."[31] Chumney drew his research from

---

30   Ibid, 26.
31   Ibid, 26.

top Messianic teachers and Jewish documents and teachings. He spent three years studying these feasts, and he reached the same conclusion that is the premise of this work. Chumney's research reveals the original Jewish teachings and practices that align with the theory of this book.

FESTIVAL OF UNLEAVENED BREAD

For *seven* days after Passover, the Jews were to eat bread without leaven.[32] Leaven represents sin. In preparation for this festival, the people were to clean their house of all leaven. This was done as part of a process to ensure there was absolutely no leaven in the home. The family would have to find the leaven and then sweep it on to a spoon with a feather. According to Chumney, the wooden spoon was symbolic of the cross, where all sin would be placed, and the feather of the Holy Spirit, who convicts the world of sin.[33] Jesus' coming allows us to clean our lives from sin and the effects of sin.

One of the steps of the Passover meal involved three pieces of unleavened bread. The middle piece was taken, broken in two, wrapped in linen and buried. This piece was later redeemed and ransomed during the meal. The children who found the buried bread received a gift, which was known as the promise of the Father.[34] This represented Jesus, whose body was broken between two thieves; he then died and was placed in linen and buried, but has now been redeemed and restored, thus offering us the gift of salvation: the promise of the Father.

FESTIVAL OF FIRST FRUITS

First fruits were the first fruits of the harvest. They symbolized

---

32   Ibid, 57.
33   Ibid, 59.
34   Ibid, 60–61.

a promise of good things to come. In this festival, God commanded the priest to wave a sheaf of the first grain of the harvest before the Lord. This was to be done on the day after the Sabbath (Leviticus 23:9–11) and took place three days after Passover. This festival fell on the exact day Jesus rose from the dead, and is thus fulfilled by the Resurrection.

Just as the people were to present the first fruit of their harvest before the Lord, Jesus was resurrected and became the "firstborn among many brothers" (Romans 8:29). When Jesus rose from the dead, He was called the firstborn and was the first fruit of God's redemptive plan for mankind. We see that after Jesus rose, many others followed him: "The tombs broke open and the bodies of many holy people who had died were raised to life. They came out of the tombs, and after Jesus' resurrection they went into the holy city and appeared to many people" (Matthew 27:52–53). The saints who died before Jesus rose from the dead were not yet able to enter Paradise because Jesus still needed to prepare the way through His death and resurrection. When he finally did rise, Jesus was the *first* to do so, and the people of God followed him. Paul actually called Jesus the "*first fruits* of those who have fallen asleep," clearly linking this festival to the salvation of the saints in Jesus (1 Corinthians 15:20).

Chumney goes into great detail to illustrate Jesus as the fulfillment of this feast: He was the firstborn of Mary (Matthew 1:23–25); the first begotten of the Father (Hebrews 1:6); the firstborn of every creature (Colossians 1:15); the first begotten of the dead (Revelation 1:5); the firstborn of many brethren (Romans 8:29); the first fruits of the resurrected ones (1 Corinthians 15:20,23); the beginning of the creation of God (Revelation 3:15); and the preeminent one (Colossians 1:18).[35]

When the Israelites presented the first sheaf of the barley

---

35 Ibid, 71–72.

harvest before the Lord, they were doing so to represent a harvest that would follow. Harvests in Scripture are prophetic symbols that represent people coming into God's kingdom. Jesus' resurrection was the first fruit of the harvest of souls that would follow!

THE FESTIVAL OF PENTECOST

This festival took place seven Sabbaths after the First Fruits. The people were to count these seven weeks off one day at a time. In the first Pentecost, fifty days after Passover and leaving Egypt, Moses met God at Mount Sinai. God revealed himself to His people in a deeper and greater way than He ever had previously.[36] The mountain was covered in <u>fire</u> and smoke.

This foreshadowed the time when exactly fifty days after Jesus was crucified on Passover, God would send His spirit through tongues of <u>fire</u>.

It is truly amazing that fifty days after Jesus died, He sent the Holy Spirit. Fifty is also the number of Jubilee that follows seven sevens. In this regard, the Jubilee Year we discussed earlier had at least a partial fulfillment in the death of Jesus and in the sending of the Holy Spirit. These events make it clear that the Lord wants to use the prophetic correlations to get our attention, thus validating the approach of this book.

For this festival, two loaves were prepared (this time with leaven). The first loaf represented Israel, which was formed and betrothed to God at Mount Sinai. The second loaf represents the church of believers that was birthed on Pentecost after Jesus rose from the dead.[37]

An interesting fact about Passover is that it occurs in the third month of the Jewish calendar. It corresponds to the sending of the Holy Spirit, while the other Spring Festivals take place in the

---

36 Ibid, 99.
37 Ibid, 94–95.

first month and are fulfilled in Jesus. In this way, this particular festival is unique. I believe this is the one festival that will take place *twice*. As it occurs in the third month, I suspect it will also fall in the third millennium following Jesus' death.

Chumney writes that there were two periods of rain in Israel: the early rain and the latter rain. This rain is a prophetic symbol for the outpouring the Spirit (see Isaiah 44:2–3 and Acts 2:17). Chumney uses Hosea 6:1–3, Joel 2:23 and James 5:7 to point out that God says Jesus' coming would be like the former *and* the latter rain. He says "The early rain refers to the outpouring of the Holy Spirit (*Ruach HaKodesh*) during *Yeshua's* first coming and the latter rain refers to the outpouring of the Holy Spirit (*Ruach HaKodesh*) during *Yeshua's* second coming."[38]

These religious festivals were a shadow of what was to come, but their reality is to be found in Christ (Colossians 2:16–17). As we have seen, the first four festivals were completely fulfilled in Jesus' death and resurrection and the subsequent sending of the Holy Spirit. In the next chapter, we will explore how the three unfulfilled festivals illustrate what will happen with the second coming.

---

38   Ibid, 97–98.

Chapter Fourteen
The (Unfulfilled) Fall Festivals

In the previous chapter, we saw that four of the seven Jewish feasts were fulfilled in Jesus' first coming. Paul wrote that all the festivals were to be fulfilled by Jesus (Colossians 2:16–17), and so we can expect with confidence that the three fall festivals will be fulfilled in the second coming. What initially struck me about these three unfulfilled festivals is that they all fell in the *seventh* month of the Jewish calendar. I do not believe this is coincidental. The unfulfilled festivals that will usher in the Second Coming and potentially the *seventh* millennium begin on the first day of the *seventh* month of the Jewish calendar.

ROSH HASHANAH – FEAST OF TRUMPETS

The Lord said to Moses, "Say to the Israelites: On the first day of the seventh month you are to have a day of rest, a sacred assembly commemorated with *trumpet blasts*. Do no regular work, but present an offering made to the Lord by fire." (Leviticus 23:23–25)

The first fall festival, which will herald Jesus' return, is Rosh HaShanah, or the Feast of Trumpets. Joel associates the blowing of trumpet with the coming of the day of the Lord (2:1; see also Joel 2:15–16). According to 1 Thessalonians 4:16–17, Jesus will return with the blast of a trumpet: "For the Lord himself will come down from heaven, with a *loud command*, with the voice of an archangel and with the *trumpet call of God*, and the dead in Christ will rise first. After that we who are still alive and are left will be caught up together with them in the clouds to meet the Lord in the air. And so we will be with the Lord forever." Paul also refers to this moment as the last trumpet saying, "We will not all sleep, but we will all be changed – in a flash, in the twinkling of an eye, at the last trumpet. For the trumpet will sound, the dead will be raised imperishable, and we will be changed" (1 Corinthians 15:51–52).

The timeline in this book suggests that Jesus will return at the beginning of the seventh millennium. We know that He will return at the blast of a trumpet. The Israelites anticipated this moment by blowing trumpet blasts *on the first day of the seventh month*, which appears to be prophetic for the beginning of the *seventh millennium*.

Chumney writes that "Jewish tradition believes that Adam was created on this day [Rosh HaShanah]."[39] As a result, even though this is the seventh month of the Biblical calendar, it is considered the first month of the new year, because it is believed to be man's first day on earth.[40] If this is true, the implication is amazing. It would make it possible for a time frame of *exactly* six thousand years (to the day) that would begin with the creation of Adam, and potentially culminate in the return of Jesus.

JERICHO AND THE FEAST OF TRUMPETS

Let's consider another Old Testament shadow God gives us: the capture of Jericho. Jericho was the first city in the Promised Land that the Israelites were to capture. The Promised Land represents

---

39 Ibid, 105.
40 Ibid, 106.

the fulfillment of the promises of God. When the Israelites go to Jericho, the Lord gives them the following instructions:

"March around the city once with all the armed men. Do this for <u>six days</u>. Have seven priests carry trumpets of rams horns in front of the ark. On the <u>seventh day</u>, march around the city seven times, with the priests *blowing the trumpets*. When you hear them sound a *long blast on the trumpets*, have all the people give a *loud shout*; the wall of the city will collapse and the people will go up, every man straight in." (Joshua 6:3–5)

For six days, the people walked once around the walls of Jericho, but the seventh day provided a total victory and the ability to enter in the city. Notice that on the seventh day, two things happened: the priests blew the trumpets and the people gave a loud shout. This is exactly what will happen when Jesus returns. As we saw in 1 Thessalonians 4:16–17, Jesus will come down from heaven with a loud shout and a trumpet blast. We will enter into his presence, and there will be no more barriers between us and God. All of this took place at Jericho on the *seventh day*. At the very least, Jericho provides a picture of <u>what</u> to expect with Jesus' return. And if a day shall be like a thousand years, Jericho also tells us <u>when</u> to expect Jesus' return.

YOM KIPPUR – DAY OF ATONEMENT

Yom Kippur is the second of the fall feasts and its fulfillment will be the physical return of Jesus to the earth. This was known as the Day of Atonement where atonement (payment) was made between the priest and God (Leviticus 23:28). This day is also known by the phrase "face to face" because it was the one day the high priest would enter into the Holy of Holies. By going past the veil in the Old Testament, the priest was entering into the manifest presence of God and meeting Him "face to face." When Jesus returns to earth, we will once again be with Him "face to face."[41]

While it began as a solemn occasion, this feast ended in celebration. There was such a sense of God's presence and cleansing of sin in Israel that single men and women would go and dance in the fields afterwards. While dancing, they would select marriage partners. This was the only time in Israel where a public espousal took place.[42] What a beautiful picture of the return of Jesus! When He does come back, we will all get to participate in a public wedding with our Lord.

What is also amazing is the link between the Year of Jubilee and the Day of Atonement. The Year of Jubilee was officially kicked off on the day of Atonement. Chumney points out:

> This was a year and a day of liberty…From Adam, it has been almost six thousand years and 120 Jubilees. The number 120 points to the end of the age of the flesh and the reign of the life of the spirit (Genesis 6:3). The ultimate fulfillment of the year of Jubilee will take place at the second coming of the Messiah. The earth will be redeemed and come into full and complete rest from the curse brought upon it by Adam's sin. Complete restoration of man's lost inheritance will take place.[43]

Chumney's observation that there are 120 Jubilees in six thousand years is very profound. If this theory holds true, then we are currently in the 120th and final Jubilee period of fifty years. Again, these prophetic numbers seem to find fulfillment in a seventh millennium initiated by the second coming of Jesus.

---

41 Ibid, 147.
42 Ibid, 148.
43 Ibid, 155.

During this feast, the Israelites were commanded to build booths that they were to live in for seven days. Historically, this feast reminded the people of their temporary dwelling in the desert, as God said, "Live in booths for seven days: All native-born Israelites are to live in booths so your descendants will know that I had the Israelites live in booths when I brought them out of Egypt" (Leviticus 23:42–43). The booth was to be a temporary dwelling place. This feast is fulfilled by the millennial reign of Jesus on earth. Prophetically, it is a picture of our dwelling with Jesus on earth for one thousand years in the Millennial Kingdom.[44]

When Jesus returns to earth, He will do so in order to dwell with us. We need to understand that time as a *temporary* dwelling with Jesus on earth, just as the booths were meant to be a *temporary* dwelling place. After the millennial reign, the first earth and the first heaven will pass away and we will then dwell permanently with God in the new heaven and the new earth (Revelation 21). I don't really know what that means, but I do know our time in the millennium with Jesus is temporary and is followed by judgment and an eternal dwelling with God in heaven.

This festival also marks the final ingathering of the harvest of crops in Israel, and thus represents the final harvest of God's children on earth.[45] This corresponds to the Millennial Reign of Christ, in which the enemy will be bound for one thousand years and those born during that period will become a great final harvest for the Lord.

The Scriptures would also seem to indicate that Jesus was

---

44 Ibid, 170.
45 Ibid, 171.

born on this feast (187).[46] A unique aspect of the booths was that they were to be built without roofs so people could observe the stars. This matters because Jesus' first coming was marked by a star. In other words, both Jesus' first and second coming will coincide with this feast.

The numerical significance of the sacrifices during this feast cannot be overlooked. During the seven days of sukkot, the number seven factored into every sacrifice. There were to be 182 sacrifices (7 x 26): 70 bulls (7 x 10), 14 rams (7 x 2), 98 lambs (7 x 14), 7 goats and 336 tenths of an ephah of flour (48 x 7). According to Chumney, "It is no coincidence that this seven-day holiday, which takes place at the height of the seventh month, had the perfect number, seven, imprinted on its sacrifices."[47] Why is God so committed to the number "seven" with this last feast? Is it because it is fulfilled in the *seventh* millennium of human history?

Finally, this is the *only* festival where the people were commanded to be joyful. Thus, this festival became known as the "season of our joy."[48] This is the last feast of the Messiah, and it will be fulfilled with the Messianic reign, which is also characterized by great joy, as we have discussed.

---

46 Ibid, 187.
47 Ibid, 174.
48 Ibid, 177

Chapter Fifteen
Every Two Thousand Years

Every two thousand years, something big happens. Two thousand years after Adam, God began a covenant through Abraham (the Old Covenant). Two thousand years later, God began a covenant through Jesus (the New Covenant). We are now on the cusp of the end of the next two thousand years, and it is my guess this will usher in an Eternal Covenant. Are we ready?

Most of us understand that the Bible is divided into two sections: the Old and New Testament. The Old Testament details the old covenant and the New Testament explains the new covenant. God instituted each of these covenants after two thousand years of history passed.

The Old Covenant began in Genesis 12 when Abraham was called by God at the age of seventy-five. At that stage, the Lord promised Abraham he would become a great nation and his people would be blessed and all the people of the earth would be blessed through him (Genesis 12:2–3). The great nation was Israel, and for the following two thousand years God was in a covenant relationship with Israel. All we understand about the Jews being the chosen people of God and about Zion and Israel began with this promise.

Two thousand years later, the covenant changed as God fulfilled the part of His promise to Abraham that *all* people would be blessed through him. Through the death and resurrection of

Jesus Christ, a new covenant was established. This made a way for all people on earth to become children of God, both Jews and Gentiles.

It is not possible to be completely accurate with the dates and so we can only make an estimation regarding the two thousand years between Adam and Abraham, and between Abraham and Jesus. Still, it is remarkable to consider that God could have followed a pattern with the establishment of His covenants with his people.

WHEN DID THE NEW COVENANT BEGIN?

The New Covenant did not begin with the birth of Jesus but rather with His death. It was only actualized after Jesus rose from the dead and after He sent the Holy Spirit. Once those things took place, God's covenant with man extended to both Jew and Gentile (or non-Jew). If the New Covenant began after Jesus rose from the dead, and if we follow a two-thousand-year pattern of covenants being established, then we are quickly approaching the next shift in history.

There are some who have anticipated a seven-thousand-year timeline but they counted the final two thousand years from Jesus' birth instead of his death. Because of this, many Christians believed the year 2000 A.D. would prompt the end of the world. They were given some support at the time by the perceived Y2K software problem that was supposed to happen at the turn of the millennium. As a result, some of these believers fell into the trap Jesus warned about of predicting a day and an hour. I strongly caution you to resist the urge to predict a day or an hour, but rather to be alert to the season we are in.

If we are going to anticipate that the second coming will fall on the third millennium (or day) following Jesus' death, then we cannot use the year 2000 A.D. Furthermore, we wouldn't know which year to look to because there is a great deal of uncertainty about the year in which Jesus actually died. Scholars assume He was approximately thirty-three years old at the time, but they do not agree about the year of His birth, nor are they sure of the year of His death. Nevertheless, it is generally thought Jesus was born between 4 and 6 BC and crucified somewhere between 27 and 33 AD.

I find it truly compelling that we cannot accurately pinpoint the date of Jesus' birth, which is the historical moment that literally split time. We count time today based on the birth of Jesus, and yet we don't know exactly when it happened. I believe this lends great weight to the theory of this book. If God has chosen to use a six-thousand-year history and to work within three two-thousand-year time frames, then knowing this and knowing the dates of Jesus' birth and death would allow for some very accurate predictions. As it is, God does not want his people predicting dates, and thus it would seem He has ordained some ambiguity surrounding these key historical events.

In his book *A Heart Ablaze,* John Bevere spends a lot of time establishing his belief that Jesus will return two thousand years after his death on the "third day." Bevere uses the passage in Exodus where God tells Moses to have the people consecrate themselves because He will be appearing on the third day (see also the second point in Chapter 10 under "third day examples"). Bevere concludes that just as the people were to consecrate themselves for two days, we have been given two thousand years (two days) to consecrate ourselves before the return of Jesus:

> We read in 2 Peter 3:8 (NKJV), "But, beloved, do not forget this one thing, that with the Lord one day is as a thousand years, and thousand years is as one day." And the psalmist wrote, "For a thousand years in Your sight are like yesterday when it is past" (Ps. 90:4 NKJV). One of God's days is a thousand of our years. So how long has it been since Jesus has been raised from the dead? The answer is, almost two

days; we are at the very end of the second day. Historians indicate that He was raised from the dead around A.D. 28 or 29. We are very close to his return, according to the prophetic time clock! We immediately see the correlation between what God said to Israel and what He is saying to us. Our responsibility as a church has been to consecrate ourselves for the past two thousand years in preparation for His coming![49]

Bevere encourages us to be ready. He further emphasizes our need to be prepared by saying:

God was saying to Israel when He told them to consecrate themselves, "I have delivered you out of Egypt. Now get Egypt out of you. This will prepare you for my coming on the beginning of the third day" …

Even so today God says to us, "I have delivered you out of the world, now get the world out of you! This will prepare you for my coming at the beginning of third thousandth year."[50]

Bevere clearly believes we are to treat a day as if it is a thousand years and we are to expect Jesus' return to come two thousand years after His resurrection. He is urging the church to be ready for Jesus' return, and he closes this chapter of his book with the following quote:

The prophet Hosea also gives us a timetable of two thousand years to prepare for His coming glory. He cried out: Come and let us return to the Lord;

---

49 John Bevere, *A Heart Ablaze* (Nashville, TN: Thomas Nelson Publishers, 1999), 27.
50 Ibid, 28.

For he has torn, but He will heal us;
He has stricken, but He will bind us up.
After two days He will revive us;
On the third day He will raise us up,
That we may live in His sight. (Hos. 6:1–2 NKJV)

After two days, two thousand years, He will revive us, and on the third thousandth year He will raise us up that we may live in His sight. The third thousandth year is the millennial reign of Christ (this is when Christ will come to earth and reign a thousand years in His gloried body [Rev. 20:4]).[51]

If the beliefs and verses above seem familiar, it is because they have already been mentioned in this book. I find it remarkable that Bevere reaches the same conclusion I have drawn, as have many others. Isaac Newton, Edward Chumney, John Bevere, Clarence Larkin[52], and Jewish theologians have all been mentioned in this work in full support of the idea that Jesus' return will come two thousand years after His Resurrection or six thousand years after Adam. Most Christian leaders I follow have a strong conviction that we are living in the end times, and they are sharing their beliefs openly. There is a strong sense among many in the Body of Christ that this is indeed the last generation. This is quite a sobering reality.

Let's go back to the pattern of covenants being established every two thousand years. Should this hold true and Jesus were to return two thousand years after his death, then we would have a new and eternal covenant established. Just as it was with the transition between the old and new covenant, the return of Christ would not abolish the previous covenants. It would fulfill

---

51 Ibid, 30.
52 See appendix with Clarence Larkin's drawing that illustrates this concept

them. We are still in the time frame that would allow for a two thousand year span between the death of Christ and His return ... between the new covenant and an eternal covenant. As we will see in the next section there is actually biblical precedent for such a pattern, and it happens to center around the timing of the first coming of Jesus.

Chapter Sixteen
Jesus' Genealogies

There are two gospels that reference Jesus' lineage: Matthew and Luke. Both are unique in the record they present, and both contain keys that would seem to confirm some of the assumptions of this book. Matthew makes it clear that God used a numerical pattern to anticipate the first coming, while Luke's gospel highlights the importance of the number seven in the coming of Jesus.

MATTHEW'S GOSPEL: 14, 14, 14

The gospel of Matthew traces Jesus' lineage from Abraham to his birth. At the end of the genealogy we find a very interesting verse: "Thus there were fourteen generations from Abraham to David, fourteen from David to the exile to Babylon, and fourteen from the exile to the Messiah" (Matthew 1:17). The fact that Matthew makes note of this pattern implies that it is significant.

What stands out immediately is that God ordained the generations perfectly from Abraham to Jesus in three sets of fourteen, with each transition being marked by a significant event. Matthew purposely points this out in his lineage because he wants us to see God's overarching hand in history leading up to Jesus' birth. The implied message is clear: this is NOT a coincidence. From Matthew's perspective, God ordered the times of the coming of

His Son, and He did so using a pattern of numbers: three sets of dates. In this way, God was able to emphasize His sovereignty as well as the importance of the coming Jesus.

This is a key that gives us insight into the prophetic nature of God. This passage of Scripture helps us to see that numbers and dates are part of God's prophetic puzzle with regard to understanding the coming of Jesus. We know that Jesus' first coming was preceded by three sets of fourteen generations. Consequently, we need to be open to the possibility presented in this book that his second coming could also be preceded by three sets of two thousand years divided by MAJOR events like the old and new covenant.

LUKE'S GOSPEL: 77 NAMES LISTED

How specific is God when it comes to prophetic numbers? Very specific, it seems. In Luke's genealogy, Jesus' lineage is traced all the way back to Adam and ultimately to God. Seventy-seven names are mentioned (Luke 3:23–38). If you include God, who is listed last, then Jesus is the seventy-seventh name. This is amazing. God seems to be making a point that the number seven factors heavily into the coming of His Son. I think it is hardly coincidental that Jesus is the seventy-seventh name mentioned. God is intentionally linking the coming of Christ with the number seven. If so, to what end? If God is that specific with the first coming of Christ, we can surely expect Him to be just as specific with the second coming.

Another point of interest we find in Luke's gospel relates to Anna. Anna was a widow and a prophetess. When someone is called to be a prophet, their life is often the message. God would often have His prophets do unusual things so they themselves would be God's word to the people. For example, God commanded Hosea to marry an unfaithful prostitute. When Hosea's wife, Gomer, left him and cheated on him, God commanded

Hosea to go after her, telling him to "show your love to your wife again, though she is loved by another and an adulteress" (Hosea 3:1). The message was clear: Even though Israel had committed adultery through idolatry, God would pursue her and love her again. Hosea's relationship with Gomer was a physical picture of this spiritual reality.

Over and over again, we see that the life of the prophet becomes the message to the people. There was one named prophet on site at the birth of Jesus – Anna. Notice what Luke's gospel says about her: "Anna was an aged widow who had been married only *seven* years before her husband passed away. After he died she chose to worship God in the temple continually. For the past *eighty-four years* she had been serving God with night-and-day prayer and fasting" (Luke 2:36–37, TPT).[53] Anna's seven years of earthly marriage before devoting her life to God's presence parallel our seven thousand years of earthly existence before eternally dwelling in God's heavenly temple.

When Anna saw Jesus, she began to praise God and to declare to everyone that the Messiah had come, a message she waited eighty-four years (7 x 12) to give. This could be a simple coincidence, or Anna's very life could be the message linking the coming of Jesus with the number seven.

Again, I would pose the question as to why the number seven and the number three are so important scripturally. They are so central to God's purposes that Jesus was the seventy-seventh name in Luke's lineage and He followed three sets of fourteen generations in Matthew's lineage. Clearly, God is wanting us to understand something about his timing! I believe He is showing us the pattern that is to be fulfilled with the most significant

---

53 This quote comes from *The Passion Translation*, which points out in the footnotes that some manuscripts say Anna was eighty-four years old, but the most reliable texts state that Anna actually spent eighty-four years in the temple.

event yet to take place – the second coming of Jesus.

Biblically, the numbers three and seven represent perfection and completion. In that way they overlap. The ultimate shadow would be if they overlap with the second coming of Jesus. If they are pointing to a seven-thousand-year history of mankind, then they are showing God's perfect and complete will for His children.

Chapter Seventeen
What Now?

If this book has produced in you a conviction that we are living in the end times and that God may have ordained a seven-thousand-year timeline, the question remains: What now? This final chapter is meant to help answer that question.

First of all, we need to understand that it is OK to have a conviction that we are living in the end times, and to respond to circumstances based on that conviction. Both Peter and Paul believed they were living in the end times and operated out of that conviction. Paul instructed people that the time was short and they should act accordingly because the world in its present form was passing away (1 Corinthians 7:29–31). We should likewise be willing to allow God to convict our hearts in this area.

We cannot fall into the trap of the scoffers that Peter prophesied would indicate the end times: "They will say, 'Where is this coming he promised? Ever since our fathers died, everything goes on as it has since the beginning of creation.'" (2 Peter 3:4). Just because others in previous generations have been convicted on this matter and appeared to be wrong does not mean we are to ignore Scripture.

1. We need to look for confirming signs.

Jesus gave us the signs of His coming for a reason (see Matthew 24 and Luke 21). The Bible prophesied His first and second coming for a reason. We need to keep an eye out for what Jesus said would happen. We are also to consider some of the biblical prophecies mentioned in this book and in others. I personally will continue to look out for signs like an increase in earthquakes and natural disasters. I will also look out for events like a one-world order, "peace" plans surrounding Israel, a one-world currency, etc. All of these are predicted end-time outcomes.

That said, people tend to see what they want to see. Let's approach future events with an open heart. They may not unfold exactly as we think they will. There were many people in the time of Jesus' first coming who knew what was supposed to happen. They also saw some of the key moments take place, but because those events looked differently than expected, they missed it. For example, their preconceived ideas of a king kept them from recognizing a baby in a manger as worthy of their worship.

Keep in mind as well that stories can be presented in many different ways. Facts can be used to report two totally different realities. An example of this might be the two completely different and seemingly factual views on global warming. We are in a very polarizing time in history, and we should not expect fulfilled prophecies to be reported on the evening news. God's Word and His Spirit needs to be our news source!

2. We should not fear.

A book like this, or anything related to this topic, can easily bring fear. We need to be on guard not to allow fear over the end times to hijack us, paralyze us or cause us to operate out of a state of paranoia. I have known some pretty fanatical people whose end-time beliefs have probably done more damage than good.

This past September (2015) was a good example. A fair bit of hysteria swept through the body of Christ because of the blood moon concept that emerged. While I do believe the blood moons are an indicator of the end times we live in, I did not begin to hoard food and water. In fact, I agreed to buy our house on the day before the Shemitah, which was when some predicted the stock markets would go into total chaos. I was not sure what would happen, but I had peace about making that big financial decision. We need to learn to own what God is saying to us *personally*, and not to live under other people's fears. For that reason, I was comfortable acting from my personal conviction. This is a skill that will serve us well in any season, but all the more so should we be approaching the culmination of the ages.

Just because someone speaks doom and gloom and uses Bible verses does not mean they are correct. They may have a valid point, but they may also have a wrong application, a wrong approach or even wrong timing. For that matter, this very book could well miss the mark in terms of application or timing. God needs to be the one to lead and direct us. I can only encourage you to allow the Holy Spirit to lead you in this area.

When it comes to being concerned about future events, we need not fear. Let me assure you, God is more than able to protect His children no matter what is happening in the world. We see such protection throughout Scripture. For example, when the ten plagues were hitting Egypt in Exodus, the Israelites were often protected. The plagues did not affect them. Look at what the Lord tells Pharaoh:

> If you do not let my people go, I will send swarms of flies on you and your officials, on your people and into your houses. The houses of the Egyptians will be full of flies, and even the ground where they are. But on that day I will deal differently with the land of Goshen, where my people live; no swarms of flies will be there, so that you will know that I, the Lord, am in this land. I will make a distinction between my people and your people. (Exodus 8:21–22)

The Lord continues to make a distinction between the live-stock of Israel and of Egypt (Exodus 9:3–4). It also did not hail in Goshen where the Israelites were (Exodus 9:26), nor did darkness affect the Israelites when it covered Egypt. This blows me away. There was darkness for three days. It was so intense that the Bible says the Egyptians could actually feel the darkness. We read that "No one could see anyone else or leave his place for three days. Yet all the Israelites had light in the places where they lived" (Exodus 10:23). This is just amazing. Finally, we read that the firstborn of the Israelites was not killed during Passover (Exodus 12:12–13).

God supernaturally protected His people, while the rest of the world was under judgment. I like to call this the Goshen princi-ple. The Israelites lived in Goshen, which is the fertile land Joseph gave his family when they came to live in Egypt. All of Egypt was in famine and suffering during the time of Joseph. The Egyptians had to give up their land, livestock and possessions and they even became slaves in order just to survive. Meanwhile, the small band of foreign Israelites was actually given the best land in the country (Genesis 47:11), and we read that they prospered there in the midst of the famine (Genesis 47:27). The Israelites experienced the exact opposite of what the Egyptians did. The Egyptians lost their land, and the Israelites gained it. The Egyptians suffered during the fam-ine, while the Israelites prospered. The Egyptians were afflicted by plagues, while the Israelites were miraculously protected. The point is this: The world can be falling apart around us and God is more than able to supernaturally preserve and prosper his people. Chumney makes the statement in his work that "The righteous will be protected during the tribulation period."[54]

If God can feed Elijah by ravens during the three-and-a-half-year drought, He can come up with creative ways to meet our

---

54 Chumney, *Seven Feasts*, 113.

needs. There is a surge of people who are joining prepper communities. They are preparing for the worst. I'm not necessarily condemning such a response. God may lay it on your heart to do likewise, but let me caution you not to do so because of fear or paranoia. I will only "prepare" for such events from a place of conviction and obedience. There is a reason why Jesus tells us six times in Matthew 6:23–34 not to fear or worry. God wants us to trust Him, and fear is a spirit that comes from the enemy. Allow His peace to guard your heart and filter anything that this book or other similar works may present.

3. We need to be ready for what God is doing in the earth.

The core message that Jesus and the New Testament writers continually emphasized was to be ready at all times. No matter what, this concept needs to guide us. Paul wrote this to the Romans: "And do this, understanding the present time. The hour has come for you to wake up from your slumber, because our salvation is nearer now than when we first believed. The night is nearly over; the day is almost here" (13:11–12). How much more true is this message today? It is not the time to slumber!

Jewish wedding customs highlight this point. In ancient times, the engagement between bride and bridegroom was the same as if they were married. This is part of what made Mary's pregnancy so problematic for Joseph. After the engagement, the bridegroom would go and prepare a place for his bride, just like Jesus said he would do for us. At the right time, when the Father of the bridegroom approved, the groom would come and get his bride. This could happen at any point in time, day or night. It was important that the bride be constantly ready because the bridegroom could come to get her in the middle of night.[55] She was

---

55   Ibid, 131–132.

constantly on watch, waiting for his return. This wedding picture parallels the second coming of Jesus. Like the Jewish bride, we are to be ready at all times.

In one of Jesus' messages on His return, he speaks of His bride (us) becoming drowsy and falling asleep (Matthew 25:5). One of the verses that should caution us in this time is this: "Because of the increase of wickedness, the love of most will grow cold, but he who stands firm to the end will be saved" (Matthew 24:12). Let's guard our love and passion for God. Let's not fall asleep or waver in our passion in this season. Part of our being ready for Jesus' return will be to stand firm to the end.

It is a lot easier to stand firm whenever I am around other encouraging, like-minded believers. We need to make sure we are standing together with other Christians. We need to guard ourselves against the increasing wickedness in the world around us. The story that comes to mind is that of putting a frog in a pot of water and slowly increasing the heat. The slow increase keeps the frog from jumping out of the pot until it is too late.

We are the bride of Christ. His coming will be anticipated by us and the Spirit, saying "Come." Let's make sure we are both awake and full of the oil of His presence. He is coming soon! Jesus final words in the Bible confirm this detail: "Yes, I am coming soon." (Revelation 22:2).

Jesus questions His followers regarding His return: "When the Son of Man comes, will he find faith on the earth?" (Luke 18:8). The answer to that question needs to be "Yes!" He wants us to be ready! If anything, I pray this book will increase our love for God and our passion to serve Him fully. May we grow in fervent passion and increased love all the more as the Day of His return approaches. May the answer to Jesus' question be a resounding "Yes" in my heart and in yours!

Appendix

The following chart was drawn by Clarence Larken nearly one hundred years ago, and is an e-sword resource. It provides a visual link between the seven days of creation and the corresponding millennium in human history.

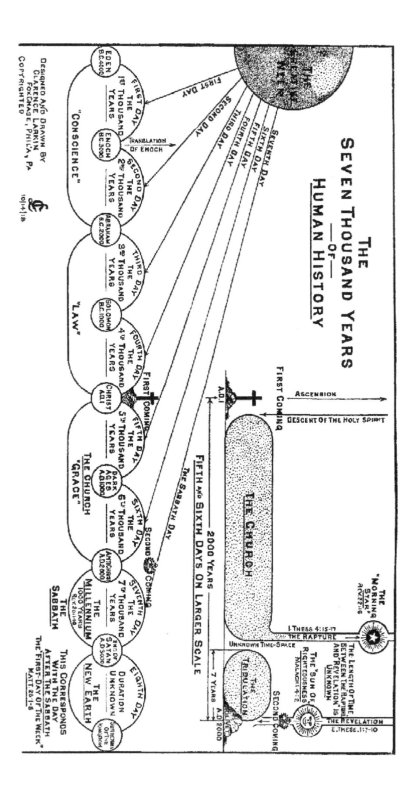

Note From the Author

It has truly been my privilege to share this work with you. I trust it has ministered to you, and blessed you as it has blessed me. I can never manage to keep books I like. I always give them away "one time too many." If you are like me, please feel free to share this with others, make copies or distribute it as the opportunity arises.

I'd love to hear from you, and can be reached at amullek@yahoo.com.

In Him,
Andrew Mullek

Made in the USA
Middletown, DE
11 May 2021